"Here we have a collection of essays and speeches by me, with breezy autobiographical commentary serving as connective tissue and splints and bandages. Here we go again with real life and opinions made to look like one big, preposterous animal not unlike an invention by Dr. Seuss..."

— Kurt Vonnegut

Fates Worse Than Death
An Autobiographical Collage

"*Fates Worse Than Death* is honest and scarily funny, and it offers a rare insight into an author who has customarily hidden his heart."

— *New York Times*

"Startlingly original...[The book] touches on actual 'fates worse than death' (Vonnegut concludes there are very few), pornography (several of his own books have been branded as such by religious zealots), Geraldo Rivera (Vonnegut's unlamented ex-son-in-law), Manhattan (Skyscraper National Park), and the fire-bombing of Dresden while he was a prisoner there during World War II (certainly the inspiration for the classic *Slaughterhouse-Five*)...Witty and warmhearted, *Fates Worse Than Death* offers a cornucopia of ideas, reminiscences, opinions, asides, anecdotes and flights of fancy. Although intensely personal, it embraces matters that touch us all."

— *St. Petersburg Times*

"An anthology in which Vonnegut freely quotes himself on everything from art and architecture to madness and mass murder ...Uncompromising."

— *Los Angeles Times*

"He remains a happy pessimist and one of the country's most thoughtful and entertaining writers."

— *San Antonio Express-News*

Books by Kurt Vonnegut

PLAYER PIANO
THE SIRENS OF TITAN
MOTHER NIGHT
CAT'S CRADLE
GOD BLESS YOU, MR. ROSEWATER
WELCOME TO THE MONKEY HOUSE
SLAUGHTERHOUSE-FIVE
HAPPY BIRTHDAY, WANDA JUNE
BREAKFAST OF CHAMPIONS
WAMPETERS, FOMA & GRANFALLOONS
SLAPSTICK
JAILBIRD
PALM SUNDAY
DEADEYE DICK
GALÁPOGOS
BLUEBEARD
HOCUS POCUS
TIMEQUAKE
FATES WORSE THAN DEATH
BAGOMBO SNUFF BOX

FATES
WORSE THAN
DEATH

AN AUTOBIOGRAPHICAL COLLAGE

KURT VONNEGUT

BERKLEY BOOKS, NEW YORK

The author gratefully acknowledges permission from the following sources to use previously published material, on the pages indicated: *Architectural Digest* (pp. 37-40); The Franklin Library (pp. 45-48, copyright © 1987, and pp. 129-130, copyright © 1990 by The Franklin Library, Franklin Center, Pennsylvania, for exclusive use in its Signed First Editions of *Bluebeard* and *Hocus Pocus*, respectively); Four Walls Eight Windows (pp. 56-59); *Lear's* (pp. 113-116, first published 1988); *The Nation* magazine/The Nation Co. Inc. (pp. 132-137, copyright © 1983); The New York Times Company (pp. 183-187, copyright © 1990 by The New York Times Company; reprinted by permission); Kroch's & Brentano's (pp. 187-188); Dell Publishing Group, Inc., and Mark Vonnegut (pp. 205-207, afterword to the 1988 edition of *The Eden Express*); and Catbird Press (pp. 210-212, from *Toward the Radical Center: A Karel Čapek Reader*, edited by Peter Kussi, translated by Dora Round, revised by Peter Kussi, copyright © 1990 by Peter Kussi and Catbird Press).

Some material appeared previously, in slightly different form, in *Architectural Digest, Esquire, Parade,* and *Time.*

The author wishes to thank Dean Brelis, John F. Collins, the Reverend Paul Jones, Tom Jones, Mary T. O'Hare, and John Updike.

This Berkley book contains the complete text of the original hardcover edition.

FATES WORSE THAN DEATH

A Berkley Book / published by arrangement with
the author

PRINTING HISTORY
G. P. Putnam's Sons edition / September 1991
Published simultaneously in Canada
Berkley trade paperback edition/ September 1992

ISBN: 0-425-13406-7

BERKLEY®
Berkley Books are published by
The Berkley Publishing Group, a division of Penguin Putnam Inc.,
375 Hudson Street, New York, New York 10014.
BERKLEY and the "B" design are trademarks
belonging to Penguin Putnam Inc.

PRINTED IN THE UNITED STATES OF AMERICA

20   19   18   17

IN MEMORY OF KURT VONNEGUT (SR.)

O God who hast hitherto supported me, enable me to proceed in this labor & in the whole task of my present state that when I shall render up at the last day an account of the talent committed to me I may receive pardon for the sake of Jesus Christ. Amen.

—SAMUEL JOHNSON,
diary entry for April 3, 1753,
when he was working on his
*Dictionary of the English Language**

*April 3, therefore, might be called "Writer's Day."

Photograph © 1973 by Jill Krementz; courtesy of the photographer

PREFACE

The adjacent photograph by Jill Krementz (my wife) shows me with the great German writer Heinrich Böll (like me and Norman Mailer and James Jones and Gore Vidal a former Private in the Infantry). We are on a sightseeing bus in Stockholm during an international congress of the writers' organization P.E.N. (Poets, Playwrights, Essayists, Editors, Novelists) in 1973. I told Böll of a German veteran of World War II (then a carpenter of my acquaintance on Cape Cod) who had shot himself in the thigh in order to get away from the Russian Front but whose wound had healed by the time he got to a hospital. (There was talk of a court-martial and a firing squad, but then the Red Army overran the hospital and took him prisoner.) Böll said that the correct way to shoot yourself was through a loaf of bread, in order to avoid powder burns. That is what we are laughing about. (The Vietnam War was going on then, during which many infantrymen surely considered wounding themselves and pretending that it had been done by an enemy.)

Later on (when we had stopped laughing) he said that the French writers Jean-Paul Sartre and Albert Camus came looking for German writers after World War II, saying in effect, "You must tell us what it was like for you." (Böll, like Sartre and Camus, would win a Nobel Prize for Literature.) In 1984, a year before Böll's death at the age of sixty-seven (one year short of my age now, and I smoke as much as he did), he invited me to take part in a dialogue about Germanness to be taped and edited for television by the BBC. I was honored. I loved the man and his work. I accepted. The program was a flop, fogbound and melancholy and mainly pointless, although it is still aired again and again on cable in this country when there is nothing else to show. (We are sort of packing material to keep a big box of junk jewelry from rattling.) I ask him what the most dangerous flaw is in the German character, and he replies, "Obedience."

Here are the last words he would ever say to me in this life (and he was on two canes and still smoking like a chimney, and about to board a taxicab to the airport in a cold London drizzle): "Oh, Koort, it is so hard, so *hard*." He was one of the last shreds of native German sorrow and shame about his country's part in World War II and its prelude. He told me off camera that he was despised by his neighbors for remembering when it was time to forget.

Time to forget.

A preface is commonly the last part of a book to be written, although it is the first thing a reader is expected to see. Six months have passed since the completion of the body of this book. Only now am I stitching this coverlet, as my editor, Faith Sale, and I prepare to put the creature to beddy-bye.

My daughter Lily has turned eight during the interval. The Russian Empire has collapsed. All the weapons we thought we might have to use on the USSR we are now applying without stint and unopposed to Iraq, a nation one-sixteenth that populous. A speech our President delivered yesterday on the subject of why we had no choice but to attack Iraq won him the highest rating in television history, a record held many years ago, I remember, by Mary Martin in *Peter Pan*. Yes, and I provided answers that same yesterday to questions put to me by a British publication, *Weekly Guardian,* with these results:

Q: What is your idea of perfect happiness?

A: Imagining that something somewhere wants us to like it here.

Q: What living person do you most admire?

A: Nancy Reagan.

Q: What is the trait you most deplore in others?

A: Social Darwinism.

Q: What vehicle do you own?

A: 1988 Honda Accord.

Q: What is your favorite smell?

A: What comes out the back door of a bakery.

Q: What is your favorite word?

A: "Amen."

Q: What is your favorite building?

A: The Chrysler Building in Manhattan.

Q: What words or phrases do you most overuse?

A: "Excuse me."

Q: When and where were you happiest?

A: About ten years ago my Finnish publisher took me to a little inn on the edge of the permafrost in his country. We took a walk and found frozen ripe blueberries on bushes. We thawed them in our mouths. It was as though something somewhere wanted us to like it here.

Q: How would you like to die?

A: In an airplane crash on the peak of Mount Kilimanjaro.

Q: What talent would you most like to have?

A: Cello.

Q: What do you consider the most overrated virtue?

A: Teeth.

K.V.
January 17, 1991

Fates Worse Than Death

I

Here we have a sequel, not that anyone has clamored for one, to a book called *Palm Sunday* (1980), a collection of essays and speeches by me, with breezy autobiographical commentary serving as connective tissue and splints and bandages. Here we go again with real life and opinions made to look like one big, preposterous animal not unlike an invention by Dr. Seuss, the great writer and illustrator of children's books, like an oobleck or a grinch or a lorax, or like a sneech perhaps.

Or a unicorn, not a Seuss invention.

(The real name of Dr. Seuss is Theodor Geisel. He was born in 1904 and I was born in 1922.)

When I went to Cornell University in 1940, I joined a fraternity (Delta Upsilon) which had murals by Dr. Seuss in its basement bar. He had drawn them in pencil long before my time. An artist in the fraternity made them bold and permanent with paint afterward.

(For those who do not know the drawings of Dr. Seuss: They depict animals with improbable numbers of joints, with crazy ears and noses and tails and feet, brightly colored usually, such as persons sometimes report seeing when suffering from delirium tremens. More commonly, I am told, people with d.t.'s see rats.)

Dr. Seuss was a Dartmouth man and not a DU, but he drew the murals while roistering in Ithaca with a painter pal, Hugh Troy, who was both a Cornellian and a DU. Troy was also a legendary player of elaborate practical jokes. (There was no money in any of his stunts. They were all *pro bono publico*.) Troy would revisit his old fraternity during my freshman year and regale me and my callow brothers with tales of his exploits.

He told us about the time he emptied a New York subway car in three stops by boarding it with a large number of friends who pretended to be strangers to one another. This was in the wee hours following New Year's Eve. Each conspirator was carrying a copy of the *Daily News* with the bold headline: HOOVER OUT, ROOSEVELT IN. Troy had saved the papers from Roosevelt's landslide victory about a year before. (That would have been back at the very start of 1934, I guess, when I was eleven years old, the fourth year of the Great Depression.)

Another time Troy bought a park bench, insisting on a bill of sale. He and a friend set it down in Central Park until a policeman appeared. Then they picked it up and ran. When the policeman caught up with them Troy showed him the bill of sale. They did this many times, until all the police in the area understood that Troy owned the bench. Then they started picking up benches belonging to the City, with the police leaving them strictly alone. They made a big pile of them somewhere in the park.

Even in my salad days (when I was green in judgment) that seemed like a dumb joke to me, a heck of a lot of work for nothing. But I listened to Troy respectfully, since I had been sent to an Ivy League college from a public school in Indianapolis in order that I might become more sophisticated. (If I had gone to Indiana University or Purdue or Wabash or DePauw, I might now be a Congressman or Senator.)

After Troy left, I experimented with becoming a practical joker myself. I went to the final examinations of several large courses in which I was not enrolled, stood up, tore the questions to pieces, threw them into the face of the instructor, and exited, slamming the door behind me. I evidently inspired many copycats, since this sort of behavior at finals became epidemic.

Success!

My final practical joke at Cornell, like my first one, made a jackass out of nobody but myself. All males were required to take two years of ROTC. I was in the horse-drawn Artillery, believe it or not. (That is how long ago that was.) By the end of my sophomore year the USA was at war with Germany, Italy, and Japan. I had enlisted in the Army and was waiting to be called. A Major General came to inspect us. I went to that inspection wearing every sort of medal, for swimming, for scouting, for Sunday-school attendance or whatever, that I could borrow from anyone. I may have been going nuts, since I was flunking practically everything, including ROTC.

The General asked my name but otherwise made no comment. I am sure, though, that he made a record of the incident, as he should have, and that his report shadowed me, as it should have, during my subsequent three years as a full-time soldier, ensuring that I, until the very end, would never rise above the rank of Private First Class. It served me right, and it was one of the best things that ever happened to me. (A half-educated PFC has so much to *think* about!)

When the war was over (forty-five years ago!), I like everybody else was entitled to wear a badge and several ribbons which were militarily correct and respectable. It is my wry satisfaction now, since I know what I did to deserve such ornaments, to regard them as no more meaningful than the borrowed trinkets I wore at that fateful ROTC inspection so long ago. The joke at the beginning was the joke at the end. How was that for foreshadowing?

And who goes to an Ivy League school in order to become a

permanent PFC? I did. (So did Norman Mailer. He has his own tale to tell.)

It was a tradition in the Indianapolis branch of our once large and cohesive family that we should go east to college but then come back to Indianapolis. My Uncle Alex went to Harvard, and his first assignment was to write an essay about why he had chosen to study there. His opening sentence, he told me, was, "I came to Harvard because my big brother is at MIT."

His big brother was my father, Kurt Sr., who was then studying architecture. Many years later, when I joined the Army as an unpromotable PFC, my father would say, "Good! They will teach you to be neat!" (He could be very funny, but he wasn't funny that time. He was grim. That is how messy I was, I guess.) He died eventually, and in an act of Freudian cannibalism, I dropped the "Jr." from my name. (Thus in lists of my works do I appear to be both my father and my son, Kurt Vonnegut and Kurt Vonnegut, Jr.) I had this to say about him in *Architectural Digest*:

"When my father was sixty-five and I was twenty-seven, I said to him, thinking him a very old man, that it must have been fun for him to be an architect. He replied unexpectedly that it had been no fun at all, since architecture had everything to do with accounting and nothing to do with art. I felt that he had mousetrapped me, since he had encouraged me up until that moment to believe that architecture for him had indeed been a lark.

"I now perceive his deception, so suddenly discontinued, as having been a high order of gallantry. While my two siblings and I were growing up, he gave us the illusion that our father was jauntily content with his professional past and excited about all the tough but amusing challenges still to come. The truth was that the Great Depression and then World War II, during which almost all building stopped, came close to gutting him as an architect. From the time he was forty-five until he was sixty-one he had almost no work. In prosperous times those would have been his best years, when his evident gifts, reputation, and maturity might have caused some imaginative client to feel that Father was entitled to reach, even in Indianapolis, for greatness or, if you will, for soul-deep fun.

"I am not about to speak of soup kitchens, much in the news again of late. We never missed a meal during the Great Depression. But Father had to close down his office, started up by *his* father, the first licensed architect in Indiana, and let his six employees go. Small jobs still came his way now and then, jobs so uninteresting, I now understand, that they would have been soporific to a high school drafting class. If we hadn't needed the money, Father might have said what I heard him say to a would-be client after World War II, when prosperity had returned to the land: 'Why don't you get some pencils and squared paper, and see what you and your wife can do?' He said this pleasantly. He was trying to be helpful.

"During the war he stopped being an architect entirely, and went to work in inventory control at the Atkins Saw Company, which was making weapons of some sort, maybe bayonets. It was then that his wife died. It became clear to him, too, that none of his three children would live in Indianapolis when the war was over. We would be following careers which would require us to live far away. So he was all but gutted yet again.

"When prosperity, but not his children, returned to Indianapolis, Father became a partner of much younger men in a new architectural firm. His reputation was still excellent, and he was one of the most universally loved men in town, a founder, by the way, of the city's now world-famous Children's Museum. He was especially admired for his design of the Bell Telephone headquarters on North Meridian Street, a project conceived before the stock market crash.

"After the war, Bell Telephone resolved to add more floors to the building, their exteriors to be identical with those of the eight below. They hired another architect, although Father was not senile or alcoholic or in any other way impaired. To

Bell Telephone, an architect was an architect. Bell got the job done and it looked OK. So much for the romance of architecture.

"Father retired alone to Brown County, Indiana, soon after that, to spend the rest of his life as a potter. He built his own potter's wheel. He died down there in the hills in 1957, at the age of seventy-two.

"When I try to remember now what he was like when I was growing up and he had so little satisfying work to do, I see him as Sleeping Beauty, dormant in a brier patch, waiting for a prince. And it is easy to jump from that thought to this one: All architects I have known, in good times or bad, have seemed to be waiting forever for a generous, loving client who will let them become the elated artists they were born to be.

"So my father's life might be seen as a particularly lugubrious fairy tale. He was Sleeping Beauty, and in 1929 not one but several princes, including Bell Telephone, had begun to hack through the briers to wake him up. But then they all got sick for sixteen years. And while they were in the hospital a wicked witch turned Sleeping Beauty into Rip Van Winkle instead.

"When the Depression hit I was taken out of private school and put into public school. So I had a new set of friends to bring home to have a look at whatever my father was. These were the ten-year-old children of the yeomanry of Hoosierdom, and it was they who first told me that my father was as exotic as a unicorn.

"In an era when men of his class wore dark suits and white shirts and monochromatic neckties, Father appeared to have outfitted himself at the Salvation Army. Nothing matched. I understand now, of course, that he had selected the elements of his costume with care, that the colors and textures were juxtaposed so as to be interesting and, finally, beautiful.

"While other fathers were speaking gloomily of coal and iron and grain and lumber and cement and so on, and yes, of Hitler and Mussolini, too, my father was urging friends and startled strangers alike to pay attention to some object close at hand, whether natural or manmade, and to celebrate it as a masterpiece. When I took up the clarinet, he declared the instrument, black studded with silver, to be a masterpiece. Never mind whether it could make music or not. He adored chess sets, although he could not play that game worth a nickel. My new friends and I brought him a moth one time, wanting to know what sort of moth it was. He said that he did not know its name, but that we could all agree wholeheartedly on this much: that it was a masterpiece.

"And he was the first planetary citizen my new friends had ever seen, and possibly the last one, too. He was no more a respecter of politics and national boundaries than (that image again) a unicorn. Beauty could be found or created anywhere on this planet, and that was that.

"AT&T has completed yet another building, this one on the island of Manhattan, near where I live. The telephone company has again done without the services of my father, who could not now be awakened in any case. AT&T hired Philip Johnson instead, a Sleeping Beauty who throughout his adult life has been tickled awake by ardent princes.

"Should I now rage at Fate for not having enabled my father to have as much fun as Mr. Johnson?

"I try to imagine my father speaking to me across the abyss between the dead and the living, and I hear him saying this: 'Do not pity me because I in my prime awaited romantic challenges which never came. If you wish to carve an epitaph on my modest headstone in Crown Hill Cemetery at this late date, then let it be this: IT WAS ENOUGH TO HAVE BEEN A UNICORN.' "

Thus ends that piece. I am moved to add that Father tried to make good times revisitable (a trick which was easy as pie for the Tralfamadorians in my novel *Slaughterhouse-Five*) by gluing cheerful documents to sheets of masonite and protecting them with varnish. Thanks to Father, this mummified letter now hangs on the wall of my workroom:

"Dear Pop:

"I sold my first story to *Collier's*. Received my check ($750 minus a 10% agent's commission) yesterday noon. It now appears that two more of my works have a good chance of being sold in the near future.

"I think I'm on my way. I've deposited my first check in a savings account and, as and if I sell more, will continue to do so until I have the equivalent of one year's pay at GE. Four more stories will do it nicely, with cash to spare (something we never had before). I will then quit this goddamn nightmare job, and never take another one so long as I live, so help me God.

"I'm happier than I've been for a good many years.

"Love."

The letter is signed with my first initial, which is what he called me. It is no milestone in literature, but it looms like Stonehenge beside my own little footpath from birth to death. The date is October 28, 1949.

Father glued a message from himself on the back of that piece of masonite. It is a quotation from *The Merchant of Venice* in his own lovely hand:

An oath, an oath, I have an oath in Heaven:
Shall I lay perjury on my soul?

II

If a maiden sits on the ground in a clearing in a forest where a unicorn lives, they say, the unicorn will come to her and put its head in her lap. That is the best way to catch a unicorn. This procedure must have been discovered by a maiden who sat down in a clearing with no intention of catching a unicorn. The unicorn with its head in her lap must have been an embarrassment. (What next?)

In the household of my childhood and youth, my sister Alice, dead for many years now (and missed like heck by me), was the maiden and our father was the elusive and spookily enchanted unicorn. My only other sibling, my own big brother who went to MIT, Bernard, and I could never catch him. To him we weren't all that interesting. As far as the two of us are concerned, this is not a remotely tragic tale. We were tough. We could take it. We had other fans.

(My daughter Edith was once married most unfortunately to a man named Geraldo Rivera who at this writing interviews little clumps of people on weekday afternoon television who have had experiences which are generally perceived as fantastic. I mention him at this point because some of these guests have been sexually abused by close relatives. I hasten to assert that my sister, five years older than I, was not remotely abused by our gentle father. Like a maiden with a unicorn's head in her lap, she was at worst merely mystified.)

Our father when I, his youngest child, got to know him was, understandably, desperate for uncritical friendship from a member of the reputedly compassionate sex, since our mother (his wife) was going insane. Late at night, and always in the privacy of our own home, and never with guests present, she expressed hatred for Father as corrosive as hydrofluoric acid. Hydrofluoric acid can eat its way out of a glass bottle, and then through a tabletop and then through the floor, and then straight to Hell.

(Actually, hydrofluoric acid can't eat through wax. A joke going around Cornell DU in my day, when most of my brothers were studying engineering of some sort, was, "If you happen to discover a universal solvent, what will you store it in?" And again actually, water is much closer to being a universal solvent than hydrofluoric acid. It just can't eat through glass.)

I made the strong suggestion in *Palm Sunday* that my mother's untreated, unacknowledged insanity was caused by bad chemicals she swallowed rather than created within herself, principally alcohol and unlimited quantities of prescribed barbiturates. (She did not live long enough to have a doctor pep her up with some sort of amphetamine.) I am willing to believe that her ailment was hereditary, but I have no American ancestors (fully accounted for in *Palm Sunday*) who were clinically crazy. In any case, what the heck? I didn't get to choose my ancestors, and I look upon my brain and the rest of my body as a house I inhabit which was built long before I was born.

(My actual house here in Manhattan was built on spec in 1862 by somebody named L. S. Brooks. It is eighteen and a half feet wide and forty-six feet deep, and three stories high. Brooks built twenty identical houses all at one whack!)

At the time of the disgraceful Bush vs. Dukakis campaign for the Presidency of the United States of America (at which time the eventual winner was promising to protect rich light people everywhere from poor dark people everywhere), I was an invited speaker at a meeting of the American Psychiatric Association in Philadelphia. My inherited brain and voicebox said this to those assembled:

"I greet you with all possible respect. It is tough to make unhappy people happier unless they need something easily prescribed, such as food or shelter or sympathetic companionship—or liberty.

"You have honored my own trade, which is the telling of stories for money, some true, some false, by inviting my friend and colleague Elie Wiesel and then me to speak to you. You may be aware of the work of Dr. Nancy Andreassen at the University of Iowa Medical Center, who interviewed professional writers on the faculty of her university's famous Writers' Workshop in order to discover whether or not our neuroses were indistinguishable from those of the general population. Most of us, myself included, proved to be depressives from families of depressives.

"From that study I extrapolate this rough rule, a very approximate rule, to be sure: You cannot be a good writer of serious fiction if you are not depressed.

"A rule we used to be able to extrapolate from cultural history, one which doesn't seem to work anymore, is that an American writer had to be an alcoholic in order to win a Nobel Prize—Sinclair Lewis, Eugene O'Neill, John Steinbeck, the suicide Ernest Hemingway. That rule no longer works, in my opinion, because artistic sensibilities are no longer regarded in this country as being characteristic of females. I no longer have to arrive at this lectern drunk, having slugged somebody in a bar last night, in order to prove that I am not what was a loathsome creature not long ago, which is to say a homosexual.

"Elie Wiesel made his reputation with a book called *Night,* which is about the horrors of the Holocaust as witnessed by the boy he used to be. I made my reputation with a book called *Slaughterhouse-Five,* which is about a British and American response to that Holocaust, which was the firebombing of Dresden—as witnessed by the young American Infantry Private First Class I used to be. We both have German last names. So does the man who invited me here, Dr. Dichter. So do most of the famous pioneers in your profession. It would not surprise me if a plurality of us here, Jews and Gentiles alike, did not have ancestors who were citizens of the German or Austro-Hungarian Empire, which gave us so much great music and science and painting and theater, and whose remnants gave us a nightmare from which, in my opinion, there can never be an awakening.

"The Holocaust explains almost everything about why Elie Wiesel writes what he writes and is what he is. The firebombing of Dresden explains absolutely nothing about why I write what I write and am what I am. I am sure you are miles ahead of me in thinking of a thousand clinical reasons for this being true. I didn't give a damn about Dresden. I didn't know anybody there. I certainly hadn't had any good times there before they burned it down. I had seen some Dresden china back home in Indianapolis, but I thought then and still think now that it's mostly kitsch. There is another wonderful gift from German-speaking people, along with psychoanalysis and *The Magic Flute*: that priceless word *kitsch.*

"And Dresden china isn't made in Dresden anyway. It's made in Meissen. That's the town they should have burned down.

"I am only joking, of course. I will say anything to be funny, often in the most horrible situations, which is one reason two good women so far have been very sorry on occasion to have married me. Every great city is a world treasure, not a national treasure. So the destruction of any one of them is a planetary catastrophe.

"Before I was a soldier I was a journalist, and that's what I was in Dresden—a voyeur of strangers' miseries. I was outside the event. Elie Wiesel, seeing what he saw—and he was just a boy, and I was a young man—was the event itself. The fire-bombing of Dresden was quick, was surgical, as the military scientists like to say, fitting the Aristotelian ideal for a tragedy, taking place in less than twenty-four hours. The Holocaust ground on and on and on and on. The Germans wanted to keep me alive, on the theory that they might be able to trade me and my captured comrades for some of their own someday. The Germans, aided and abetted, of course, by like-minded Austrians and Hungarians and Slovaks and French and Ukrainians and Romanians and Bulgarians and so on, wanted Elie Wiesel and everyone he had ever known, and everyone remotely like him, to die, as his father would die, of malnutrition, overwork, despair, or cyanide.

"Elie Wiesel tried to keep his father alive. And failed. My own father, and most of the rest of my friends and loved ones, were safe and sound in Indianapolis. The proper prescription for the fatal depression which killed Elie Wiesel's father would have been food and rest and tender loving care rather than lithium, Thorazine, Prozac, or Tofranil.

"I hold a master's degree in anthropology from the University of Chicago. Students of that branch of poetry are taught to seek explanations for human comfort or discomfort—wars, wounds, spectacular diseases, and natural disasters aside—in culture, society, and history. And I have just named the villains in my books, which are never individuals. The villains again: culture, society, and history—none of them strikingly housebroken by lithium, Thorazine, Prozac, or Tofranil.

"Like most writers, I have at home the beginnings of many books which would not allow themselves to be written. About twenty years ago, a doctor prescribed Ritalin for me, to see if that wouldn't help me get over such humps. I realized right away that Ritalin was dehydrated concentrate of pure paranoia, and threw it away. But the book I was trying to make work was to be called *SS Psychiatrist*. This was about an MD who had been psychoanalyzed, and he was stationed at Auschwitz. His job was to treat the depression of those members of the staff who did not like what they were doing there. Talk therapy was all he or anybody had to offer back then. This was before the days of— Never mind.

"My point was, and maybe I can make it today without having to finish that book, that workers in the field of mental health at various times in different parts of the world must find themselves asked to make healthy people happier in cultures and societies which have gone insane.

"Let me hasten to say that the situation in our own country is nowhere near that dire. The goal here right now, it seems to me, is to train intelligent, well-educated people to speak stupidly so that they can be more popular. Look at Michael Dukakis. Look at George Bush.

"I think I was invited here mostly because of what happened to my dear son Mark Vonnegut, now Dr. Vonnegut. He had a very fancy crack-up, padded-cell stuff, straitjacket stuff, hallucinations, wrestling matches with nurses, and all that. He recovered and wrote a book about it called *The Eden Express,* which is about to be reissued in paperback by Dell, with a new Afterword by him. You should have hired him instead of me. He would have been a heck of a lot cheaper, and he knows what he is talking about.

"He speaks well. When he lectures to mental health specialists, he always asks a question at one point, calling for a show of hands. I might as well be his surrogate and ask the same question of you. A show of hands, please: How many of you have taken Thorazine? Thank you. Then he says, 'Those who haven't tried it really should. It won't hurt you, you know.'

"He was diagnosed, when I took him to a private laughing academy in British Columbia, where he had founded a commune, as schizophrenic. He sure looked schizophrenic to me, too. I never saw depressed people act anything like that. We mope. We sleep. I have to say that anybody who did what Mark did shortly after he was admitted, which was to jump up and get the light bulb in the ceiling of his padded cell, was anything but depressed.

"Anyway—Mark recovered sufficiently to write his book and graduate from Harvard Medical School. He is now a pediatrician in Boston, with a wife and two fine sons, and two fine automobiles. And then, not very long ago, most members of your profession decided that he and some others who had written books about recovering from schizophrenia had been misdiagnosed. No matter how jazzed up they appeared to be when sick, they were in fact depressives. Maybe so.

"Mark's first response to news of this rediagnosis was to say, 'What a wonderful diagnostic tool. We now know if a patient gets well, he or she definitely did not have schizophrenia.'

"But he, too, unfortunately, will say anything to be funny. A more sedate and responsible discussion by him of what was wrong with him can be found in the Afterword to the new edition of his book. I have a few copies of it, which I hope somebody here will have xeroxed, so that everyone who wants one can have one.

"He isn't as enthusiastic about megavitamins as he used to be, before he himself became a doctor. He still sees a whole lot more hope in biochemistry than in talk.

"Long before Mark went crazy, I thought mental illness was caused by chemicals, and said so in my stories. I've never in a story had an event or another person drive a character crazy. I thought madness had a chemical basis even when I was a boy, because a close friend of our family, a wise and kind and wryly sad man named Dr. Walter Bruetsch, who was head of the State's huge and scary hospital for the insane, used to say that his patients' problems were chemical, that little could be done for them until that chemistry was better understood.

"I believed him.

"So when my mother went crazy, long before my son went crazy, long before I had a son, and finally killed herself, I blamed chemicals, and I still do, although she had a terrible childhood. I can even name two of the chemicals: phenobarbital and booze. Those came from the outside, of course, the phenobarbs from our family doctor, who was trying to do something about her sleeplessness. When she died, I was a soldier, and my division was about to go overseas.

"We were able to keep her insanity a secret, since it became really elaborate only at home and between midnight and dawn. We were able to keep her suicide a secret thanks to a compassionate and possibly politically ambitious coroner.

"Why do people try so hard to keep such things a secret? Because news of them would make their children seem less attractive as marriage prospects. You now know a lot about my family. On the basis of that information, those of you with children contemplating marriage might be smart to tell them: Whatever you do, don't marry anybody named Vonnegut.

"Dr. Bruetsch couldn't have helped my mother, and he was the greatest expert on insanity in the whole State of Indiana. Maybe he knew she was crazy. Maybe he didn't. If he did know she was crazy after midnight, and he was very fond of her, he must have felt as helpless as my father. There was not then an Indianapolis chapter of Alcoholics Anonymous, which might have helped. One would be founded by my father's only brother, Alex, who was an alcoholic, in 1955 or so.

"There—I've told you another family secret, haven't I? About Uncle Alex?

"Am I an alcoholic? I don't think so. My father wasn't one. My only living sibling, my brother, isn't one.

"But I am surely a great admirer of Alcoholics Anonymous, and Gamblers Anonymous, and Cocaine Freaks Anonymous, and Shoppers Anonymous, and Gluttons Anonymous, and on and on. And such groups gratify me as a person who studied anthropology, since they give to Americans something as essential to health as vitamin C, something so many of us do not have in this particular civilization: an extended family. Human beings have almost always been supported and comforted and disciplined and amused by stable lattices of many relatives and friends until the Great American Experiment, which is an experiment not only with liberty but with rootlessness, mobility, and impossibly tough-minded loneliness.

"I am a vain person, or I would not be up here, going 'Blah, blah, blah.' I am not so vain, however, as to imagine that I have told you anything you didn't already know—except for the trivia about my mother, my Uncle Alex, and my son. You deal with unhappy people hour after hour, day after day. I keep out of their way as much as possible. I am able to follow the three rules for a good life set down by the late writer Nelson Algren, a fellow depressive, and another subject of the study of writers made at the University of Iowa. The three rules are, of course: Never eat at a place called Mom's, never play cards with a man named Doc, and most important, never go to bed with anybody who has more troubles than you do.

"All of you, I am sure, when writing a prescription for mildly depressed patients, people nowhere as sick as my mother or my son were, have had a thought on this order: 'I am so sorry to have to put you on the outside of a pill. I would give anything if I could put you inside the big, warm life-support system of an extended family instead.' "

That was the end of my speech to all those mental health workers in Philadelphia. They said afterward that I had *shared,* and that they hadn't expected me to *share* (i.e., to spill the beans about myself and my own family). I had with me copies of my son's own comments on his scary case, which I passed out to anyone interested. They can be found as well in the Appendix to this book, where I have put a lot of other stuff which, if not so segregated, might slow us down. (I have also sped things up by putting digressions, asides, non sequiturs, dialyses, epicrises, meioses, antiphrases, and so on in parentheses.)

III

When my mother went off her rocker late at night, the hatred and contempt she sprayed on my father, as gentle and innocent a man as ever lived, was without limit and pure, untainted by ideas or information. I have seen and heard hatred that pure coming from women maybe ten times since she died on Mother's Day in 1944 (about a month before D Day). I don't think the hatred has much to do with the particular man who gets it. Father surely didn't deserve it. Most likely, it seems to me, it is a response to aeons of subjugation, although my mother and all the other women who have displayed it for my supposed benefit were about as enslaved as Queen Elizabeth or Cleopatra.

My theory is that all women have hydrofluoric acid bottled up inside, but my mother had too much of it. When the clock struck midnight (and we really did have a grandfather clock which struck the hours with authority), out it came. For her it was like throwing up. She had to do it. Poor soul! Poor soul!

This is a self-serving theory, insinuating that Father and I did not deserve to be so hated. Forget it. When I was in Prague about four years before the Artists overthrew the Communists, a local writer told me that Czechs love to build elaborate theories so closely reasoned as to seem irrefutable and then, self-mockingly, to knock them down. I do that, too. (My favorite Czech writer is Karel Čapek, whose magical essay on literature I have thrown into the Appendix as proof that I am correct to be so charmed by him.)

But to get back to the thing between my father and my sister, the unicorn and the maiden: Father, no more a Freudian than Lewis Carroll, made Alice his principal source of encouragement and sympathy. He made the most of an enthusiasm they had in common, which was for the visual arts. Alice was just a girl, remember, and aside from the embarrassment of having a unicorn lay its head in her lap, so to speak, she was traumatized mainly by having every piece of sculpture or picture she made celebrated by Father as though it were Michelangelo's *Pietà* or the ceiling of the Sistine Chapel. In later life (which was going to last only until she was forty-one) this made her a lazy artist. (I have often quoted her elsewhere as saying, "Just because people have talent, that doesn't mean they have to *do* something with it.")

"My only sister, Alice," I wrote, again in *Architectural Digest,* "possessed considerable gifts as a painter and sculptor, with which she did next to nothing. Alice, who was six feet tall and a platinum blonde, asserted one time that she could roller-skate through a great museum like the Louvre, which she had never seen and which she wasn't all that eager to see, and which she in fact would never see, and fully appreciate every painting she passed. She said that she would be hearing these words in her head above the whir and clack of her wheels on the terrazzo: 'Got it, got it, got it.'

"I have subsequently discussed this with artists who are a lot more productive and famous than she was, and they have said that they, too, can almost always extract all the value from an unfamiliar painting in a single *pow*. Or, if the painting is without value, then they get no *pow*.

"And I think yet again about my father, who struggled to become a painter after he was forced into early and unwelcome retirement by the Great Depression. He had reason to be optimistic about this new career, since the early stages of his pictures, whether still lifes or portraits or landscapes, were full of *pow*. Mother, meaning to be helpful, would say of each one: 'That's really wonderful, Kurt. Now all you have to do is *finish* it.' He would then ruin it. I remember a portrait he did of his only brother, Alex, who was an insurance salesman, which he called *Special Agent*. When he roughed it in, his hand and eye conspired with a few bold strokes to capture several important truths about Alex, including a hint of disappointment. Uncle Alex was a proud graduate of Harvard, who would rather have been a scholar of literature than an insurance man.

"When Father finished the portrait, made sure every square inch of masonite had its share of paint, Uncle Alex had disappeared entirely. We had a drunk and lustful Queen Victoria instead.

"This was terrible.

"Now then: The most notorious interrupter of a masterpiece in progress, surely, was 'the person on business from Porlock,' who broke for all eternity the concentration of Samuel Taylor Coleridge on his poem *Kubla Khan*. But if there had been such a person to intrude regularly on my father in the deathly still attic of our house in Indianapolis during the Great Depression, Father might now be remembered as a minor Hoosier painter— as well, let it be said, as a good father and fine architect.

"And I will argue that interruptions are commonly beneficial, once a work of art is well begun. I myself, when reading a novel or watching a play or a film, with many chapters or scenes still to come, hear my brain saying a variation on my sister's 'Got it, got it, got it,' which is, 'End it, end it, end it. For the love of God, please end it now.' Yes, and after I have written only about two-thirds of a novel or play of my own, I suddenly feel silly and relieved, as though I were running before the wind in a little sailboat, and headed home.

"I have done all I hoped to do, and more, if I've been really lucky, than when I put to sea.

"That confession will seem as damning and barbarous to humorless persons as my sister's fantasy of whizzing through the Louvre on roller skates. At least it has the virtue of truthfulness. And I beg them to forget my own jerry-built creations, and to consider instead the tragedy of *Hamlet,* by William Shakespeare, act 3, scene 4—with two more acts, nine more scenes, to go. Hamlet has just killed the innocent, faithful, tiresome old man Polonius, having mistaken him for his mother's new husband. He discovers who it is that he has murdered, and declares with emotions which are mixed, to say the least: 'Thou wretched, rash, intruding fool, farewell!'

"Got it, got it, got it. All freeze. Bring in a person from Porlock. Lower the curtain. The play is done.

"Even in an essay as short as this one, what I will call the 'Two-thirds of a Masterpiece Is More Than Enough' rule is often applicable. I've had only one point to make, and I've made it. I will do what my mother called 'finishing it,' which, if I am not going to unmake the point again, has to be as empty as talk at the end of a party, on the order of 'Goodness, look how late it is' and 'It seems we've run out of ice' and 'Do you remember where you put your coat?' and so on.

"There is a formula for a well-made three-act play, which came from I know not where, which goes like this: 'First act, question mark. Second act, exclamation point. Third act, period.' And since normal people want only question marks and exclamation points for works of art of every sort, I place as much value on a period as on the painting careers of my father and my sister, which is zero—zip.

"As for the person from Porlock on his quotidian errand, and what he did to Coleridge: I have to ask if he deprived poetry lovers of anything. Coleridge had committed thirty lines to paper before the wretched, rash, intruding fool crashed in, and toward the bottom was this:

> *A damsel with a dulcimer*
> *In a vision once I saw:*
> *It was an Abyssinian maid,*
> *And on her dulcimer she played,*
> *Singing of Mount Abora.*

A dulcimer is a glockenspiel shaped like a trapezium, an ugly shape if there ever was one.

"If the person from Porlock had been my servant, and I had known exactly what Coleridge was doing on the other side of the door, I would have sent him in the instant the poet had written only this much:

> *In Xanadu did Kubla Khan*
> *A stately pleasure-dome decree:"*

(And there that piece ends, having said all it had to say at the two-thirds mark.)

I myself make pictures from time to time. A typical lithograph by me appears on the title page of the Appendix. I actually had a one-person show of drawings a few years back (1980) in Greenwich Village, not because my pictures were any good but because people had heard of me.

I took a photograph of my wife, Jill Krementz, for the jacket of a book by her. She set the camera and told me where to stand and how to click it. When the book came out, with my name under the picture, a gallery owner offered me a one-person show of my photographs. It wouldn't have been just a one-person show. It would have been a one-photograph show. Such is celebrity. Eat your heart out.

(I am the third member of the American branch of my family, after my daughters Nanette Prior and Edith Squibb, to have a one-person show. I am the second, after my son Mark, to spend any time whatsoever in a laughing academy. I am the first to divorce and remarry. I will say more later on about my committing myself to a bughouse for a short stay. That is quite a bit in the past now, three or four books ago.)

I would eventually write a book about a painter, *Bluebeard.* I got the idea for it after *Esquire* asked me for a piece about the Abstract Expressionist Jackson Pollock. The magazine was putting together a fiftieth-anniversary issue to consist of essays on fifty native-born Americans who had made the biggest difference in the country's destiny since 1932. I wanted Eleanor Roosevelt but Bill Moyers already had her.

(Truman Capote, a summertime neighbor of mine on Long Island, promised to write about Cole Porter. But then, at the last possible moment, he handed in an essay on my Manhattan neighbor Katharine Hepburn, take it or leave it. *Esquire* took it.)

"Jackson Pollock (1912–1956)," I wrote, "was a painter who, during his most admired period, beginning in 1947, would spread a canvas on his studio floor and dribble or spatter or pour paint on it. He was born in Cody, Wyoming, which is named in honor of a legendary creator of dead animals, 'Buffalo Bill' Cody. Buffalo Bill died of old age. Jackson Pollock came east to the State of New York, where he died violently at the age of forty-four, having, as the foremost adventurer in the art movement now known as Abstract Expressionism, done more than any other human being to make his nation, and especially New York City, the unchallenged center of innovative painting in all this world.

"Until his time, Americans were admirable for their leadership in only one art form, which was jazz. Like all great jazz musicians, Pollock made himself a champion and connoisseur of the appealing accidents which more formal artists worked hard to exclude from their performances.

"Three years before Pollock killed himself and a young woman he had just met, by driving his car into a tree on a quiet country road, he had begun to move away in his work from being what one critic called 'Jack the Dripper.' He was laying on much of the paint with a brush—again. He had started out with a brush, and as an enemy of accidents. Let it be known far and wide, and especially among the Philistines, that this man was capable of depicting in photographic detail the crossing of the Delaware by the Father of our Country, if such a tableau had been demanded by the passions of himself and his century. He had been meticulously trained in his craft by, among others, that most exacting American master of representational art, a genius of antimodernism, Thomas Hart Benton.

"Pollock was a civilian throughout World War II, although in the prime of life. He was rejected for military service, possibly because of his alcoholism, which he would conquer from time to time. He went without a drink, for example, from 1948 through 1950. He continued to paint and teach and study during the war, when the careers of so many of his American colleagues were disrupted, and when painters his own age in Europe had been forbidden by dictators to paint as they pleased, and used as fodder for cannons and crematoria and so on.

"So—while Pollock is notorious for having broken with the past, he was one of the few young artists who during the war pondered art history uninterruptedly and in peace speculated as to what the future of art might be.

"He should be astonishing even to people who do not care about painting—for this reason: He surrendered his will to his unconscious as he went about his job. He wrote this in 1947, eight years after the death of Sigmund Freud: 'When I am *in* my painting, I'm not aware of what I am doing.' It might be said that he painted religious themes during a time of enthusiasm in the Occident for peace and harmony to be found, supposedly, in a state which was neither sleep nor wakefulness, to be achieved through meditation.

"He was unique among founders of important art movements, in that his colleagues and followers did not lay on paint as he did. French Impressionists painted a lot alike, and Cubists painted a lot alike, and were supposed to, since the revolutions in which they took part were, for all their spiritual implications, quite narrowly technical. But Pollock did not animate a school of dribblers. He was the only one. The artists who felt themselves at least somewhat in his debt made pictures as madly various as the wildlife of Africa—Mark Rothko and Willem de Kooning and James Brooks and Franz Kline and Robert Motherwell and Ad Reinhardt and Barnett Newman and on and on. Those named, by the way, were personal friends of Pollock's. All vigorous schools of art, it would seem, start with artificial extended families. What bonded Pollock's particular family was not agreement as to what, generally, a picture should look like. Its members were unanimous, though, as to where inspiration should come from: the unconscious, that part of the mind which was lively, but which caught no likenesses, had no morals or politics, and had no tired old stories to tell yet again.

"James Brooks, at seventy-seven a dean of the movement, described in conversation with me the ideal set of mind for a painter who wishes to link his or her hands to the unconscious, as Pollock did: 'I must lay on the first stroke of paint. After that, I insist that the canvas do at least half the work.'

"The canvas, which is to say the unconscious, considers that first stroke, and then it tells the painter's hand how to respond to it—with a shape of a certain color and texture at that point there. And then, if all is going well, the canvas ponders this addition and comes up with further recommendations. The canvas becomes a Ouija board.

"Was there ever a more cunning experiment devised to make

the unconscious reveal itself? Has any psychological experiment yielded a more delightful suggestion than this one: that there is a part of the mind without ambition or information, which nonetheless is expert on what is beautiful?

"Has any theory of artistic inspiration ever urged painters so vehemently, while they worked, to ignore life itself—to ignore life utterly? In all the Abstract Expressionist paintings in museums and on the walls of art lovers, and in the vaults of speculators, there is very little to suggest a hand or a face, say, or a table or a bowl of oranges, or a sun or a moon—or a glass of wine.

"And could any moralist have called for a more appropriate reaction by painters to World War II, to the death camps and Hiroshima and all the rest of it, than pictures without persons or artifacts, without even allusions to the blessings of Nature? A full moon, after all, had come to be known as a 'bomber's moon.' Even an orange could suggest a diseased planet, a disgraced humanity, if someone remembered, as many did, that the Commandant of Auschwitz and his wife and children, under the greasy smoke from the ovens, had had good food every day.

"Most art movements during this fashion-crazy century have lasted as long as June bugs. A few have had life spans equivalent to those of horses or dogs. Now, more than a quarter of a century after the death of Jackson Pollock, there are more enthusiastic Abstract Expressionists than ever before, and good ones. And let it be known far and wide, and especially among the Philistines, that all this experimentation has proved that only one sort of person can produce an impressive painting by using a canvas for a Ouija board: a marvelously gifted person, as technically skilled and respectful of art history as was the now legendary 4-F from Cody.

"Willem de Kooning, a greater painter, possibly, and a European by birth besides, said this of Pollock: 'Jackson broke the ice.' "

The end. Hokay?

I sounded more enthusiastic about Pollock's dribble paintings than I really was. (Dishonest!) And I am a person who has spent a lot of his life in commercial galleries and art museums. I have done what my Abstract Expressionist pal Syd Solomon said we had to do if we wanted to tell a good painting from a bad one, which was this: "look at a million paintings first." After doing that, he said, we could never be mistaken.

My main reason for not liking the dribbles much, except possibly as textile designs, is primitive: They show me no horizon. I can easily do without information in a painting except for one fact, which my nervous system, and maybe the nervous system of all earthbound animals, insists on knowing: where the horizon is. I think of newborn deer, who have to struggle to their feet and maybe start running for their lives almost immediately. The first piece of important information their eyes transmit to their brains, surely, is the location of the horizon. So it is, too, with human beings awakening from sleep or a coma: the first thing they have to know before reasoning is where the horizon is.

As responsible shippers say on packages containing objects which are easily distressed, like the human nervous system:

THIS SIDE UP

The Franklin Library asked me to provide a special preface to its expensive edition of *Bluebeard* (illustrated by my daughter Edith Squibb). So I blathered on some more about painting, which my father and I both did badly:

"To all my friends and relatives in Alcoholics Anonymous," I began, "I say that they were right to become intoxicated. Life without moments of intoxication is not worth 'a pitcher of spit,' as the felicitous saying goes. They simply chose what was for them a deadly poison on which to get drunk.

"Good examples of harmless toots are some of the things children do. They get smashed for hours on some strictly limited aspect of the Great Big Everything, the Universe, such as water or snow or mud or colors or rocks (throwing little ones, looking under big ones), or echoes or funny sounds from the voicebox or banging on a drum and so on. Only two people are involved: the child and the Universe. The child does a little something to the Universe, and the Great Big Everything does something funny or beautiful or sometimes disappointing or scary or even painful in return. The child teaches the Universe how to be a good playmate, to be nice instead of mean.

"And professional picture painters, who are what a lot of this made-up story is about, are people who continue to play children's games with goo, and dirt, with chalks and powdered minerals mixed with oil and dead embers and so on, dabbing, smearing, scrawling, scraping, and so on, for all their natural lives. When they were children, though, there was just they and the Universe, with only the Universe dealing in rewards and punishments, as a dominant playmate will. When picture painters become adults, and particularly if other people depend on them for food and shelter and clothing and all that, not forgetting heat in the wintertime, they are likely to allow a third player, with dismaying powers to hold up to ridicule or reward grotesquely or generally behave like a lunatic, to join the game. It is that part of society which does not paint well, usually, but which knows what it likes with a vengeance. That third player is sometimes personified by an actual dictator, such as Hitler or Stalin or Mussolini, or simply by a critic or curator or collector or dealer or creditor, or in-laws.

"In any case, since the game goes well only when played by two, the painter and the Great Big Everything, *three's a crowd.*

"Vincent van Gogh excluded that third player by having no dependents, by selling no paintings save for a few to his loving brother, Theo, and by conversing as little as possible. Most painters are not that lucky, if you want to call that much solitude luck.

"Most good painters I have known wish that they did not

have to sell their pictures. The graphic artist Saul Steinberg said to me with whimsical smugness one time that he got to keep most of his creations, even after he had been paid well for them. Most of them are models for reproductions in books and magazines and poster shops, and need have no public life of their own. Steinberg makes a living from copies, but keeps the originals.

"Both my grown daughters make pictures and sell them. But they wish they could keep them. It is the third player who forces them to put them up for adoption. And that player is full of vehement advice about how to make their pictures more adoptable, how to run a successful baby factory, so to speak.

"The younger of those daughters is married to a painter who was poor for a long time, but who now is having what is called success. What do he and she find most exciting about this new affluence? It means that they can now *keep* their best pictures for themselves. They, too, can be collectors.

"My point is this: The most satisfied of all painters is the one who can become intoxicated for hours or days or weeks or years with what his or her hands and eyes can do with art materials, and let the rest of the world go hang.

"And may I say parenthetically that my own means of making a living is essentially clerical, and hence tedious and constipating. Intruders, no matter how ill-natured or stupid or dishonest, are as refreshing as the sudden breakthrough of sunbeams on a cloudy day.

"The making of pictures is to writing what laughing gas is to Asian influenza.

"As for the founders of the Abstract Expressionist movement in this country soon after World War II: The third player crashed into their privacy suddenly, and especially into that of the shy and dead-broke Jackson Pollock, with a bewildering uproar equivalent to that of a raid by the Vice Squad. Pollock was goofing around with spatters and dribbles of paint on canvas on his own time and at his own expense and on the advice of nobody, wondering, as indeed a child might, whether the result would be interesting.

"And it was.

"That was his first masterstroke, surely, something of which a child would be wholly incapable: recognizing how enchanting to adult minds pictures made in this fashion might be. His second masterstroke was to trust his intuition to control his hands so as to show, doing now this with this and then that with that, how mysteriously whole and satisfying such pictures might be.

"Some people were very upset with him, feeling that he was a swindler or a mountebank, although getting really mad at a painting or any work of art makes about as much sense as getting really mad at a banana split. Some of his supporters were at least as disconcerting, declaring that he had made an extraordinary breakthrough, in scale with the discovery of penicillin, say. He and some of his painter pals were onto something big and should keep pushing ahead. Everybody would be watching now.

"And this was sensational news in terms of money and fame to come. But it was also hellish noise to a person as shy and innocent as Jackson Pollock of Cody, Wyoming. He died young and drunk and by all reports desperately unhappy—in an automobile crash which was his own fault if not of his own making. I did not know him, but I dare to suggest an epitaph for his stone in Green River Cemetery, to wit:

THREE'S A CROWD."

(Paint and weapons have more in common than I previously realized. They both suggest to their owners surprising and possibly noteworthy things which might be done with them.)

IV

And listen to this:

"No matter where I am, and even if I have no clear idea where I am, and no matter how much trouble I may be in, I can achieve a blank and shining serenity if only I can reach the very edge of a natural body of water. The very edge of anything from a rivulet to an ocean says to me: 'Now you know where you are. Now you know which way to go. You will soon be home now.'

"That is because I made my first mental maps of the world, in the summertime when I was a little child, on the shores of Lake Maxincuckee, which is in northern Indiana, halfway between Chicago and Indianapolis, where we lived in the wintertime. Maxincuckee is three miles long and two and a half miles across at its widest. Its shores are a closed loop. No matter where I was on its circumference, all I had to do was keep walking in one direction to find my way home again. What a confident Marco Polo I could be when setting out for a day's adventure!

"Yes, and I ask the reader of this piece, my indispensable

collaborator: Isn't your deepest understanding of time and space and, for that matter, destiny shaped like mine by your earliest experiences with geography, by the rules you learned about how to get home again? What is it that can make you feel, no matter how mistakenly, that you are on the right track, that you will soon be safe and sound at home again?

"The closed loop of the lakeshore was certain to bring me home not only to my own family's unheated frame cottage on a bluff overlooking the lake, but to four adjacent cottages teeming with close relatives. The heads of those neighboring households, moreover, my father's generation, had also spent their childhood summertimes at Maxincuckee, making them the almost immediate successors there to the Potawatomi Indians. They even had a tribal name for themselves, which sounded like 'Epta-mayan-hoys.' Sometimes my father, when a grown man, would call out to Maxincuckee in general, *'Epta-mayan-hoy?'* And a first cousin fishing from a leaky rowboat or a sister reading in a hammock, or whatever, would give this reply: *'Ya! Epta-mayan-hoy!'* What did it mean? It was pure nonsense from their childhoods. It was German, if not transliterated as I have done, meaning this: 'Do abbots mow hay? Yes! Abbots mow hay!'

"So what? So not very much, I guess, except that it allows me to say that after the Potawatomis came the Epta-mayan-hoys, who have vanished from Lake Maxincuckee without a trace. It is as though they had never been there.

"Am I sad? Not at all. Because everything about that lake was imprinted on my mind when it held so little and was so eager for information, it will be my lake as long as I live. I have no wish to visit it, for I have it all right here. I happened to see it last spring from about six miles up, on a flight from Louisville to Chicago. It was as emotionally uninvolving as a bit of dry dust viewed under a microscope. Again: That wasn't the real Maxincuckee down there. The real one is in my head.

"The one in my head is the one I swam across, all two and one-half miles of it, when I was eleven years old, with my sister, five years older than me, and my brother, nine years older than me, in a leaky rowboat near me, urging me on. My sister died thirty years ago. My brother, an atmospheric scientist, is still going strong, daydreaming about clouds and electricity. Times change, but my lake never will.

"If I were ever to write a novel or a play about Maxincuckee, it would be Chekhovian, since what I saw were the consequences of several siblings' inheriting and trying to share a single beloved property, and with their own children, once grown, moving to other parts of the world, never to return, and on and on. Our cottage, owned jointly and often acrimoniously by my father and his brother and his sister, was sold to a stranger at the end of World War II. The buyer put off taking possession for a week in order that I, just married after being discharged from the Army, might take my bride there for a honeymoon. He was Concert Master of the Indianapolis Symphony Orchestra, and so must have been a romantic man. My bride, whose name was Jane Cox and who was of English ancestry, confided in me that one of her own relatives had asked her, 'Do you really want to get mixed up with all those Germans?'

"Jane has gone to Heaven, too, now, like my sister. She had me read *The Brothers Karamazov* during our honeymoon. She considered it the greatest of all novels. It was appropriate reading for a farewell visit to an old family property, since it was all about the state of people's portable souls and accorded no importance to immovable real estate.

"It was chilly but sunny. It was late autumn then.

"We went out in an old, leaky rowboat, which all my life I had called 'The Beralikur,' a mixture of my first name with those of my siblings, Bernard and Alice. But that name was not painted on the boat, which would have been redundant. Everybody who was anybody at Maxincuckee already knew that the name of that leaky boat was the Beralikur.

" 'I swam all the way across this lake when I was eleven years old,' I said to Jane.

" 'You told me,' she said.

"And I said, 'I don't think you believe I could really do a thing like that. I can't believe it, so why should you? But you ask my brother and sister if it isn't true.'

"Jane was a writer, too, by the way. *Angels Without Wings,* a book she wrote about raising all our kids on Cape Cod, was published posthumously last autumn, forty-two years exactly after our honeymoon.

"She asked me on our honeymoon what influence Culver Military Academy, which I haven't even mentioned, had on my thinking when I was a child. It was at the head of the lake, after all, and was the principal employer of the town, which is also called Culver. It was like a little West Point and Annapolis combined, with a Cavalry troop and a big fleet of sailboats and noisy parades and so on. They fired a cannon every night at sunset.

" 'I thought about it when they fired the cannon,' I said, 'and hoped I would never be sent there. I didn't want to be yelled at and have to wear a uniform.'

"A loon popped up to the surface of Lake Maxincuckee during our honeymoon, and gave its chilling, piercing, liquid cry of seeming lunacy.

"Only now do I realize that my answer should have been this: *'Ya! Epta-mayan-hoy!'*

"I lived on Cape Cod for twenty years, and so caused to be imprinted on the minds of my own children all there is to know and feel about the harbor at Barnstable and the marsh it feeds at high tide and, only two hundred yards from our house, a very deep puddle made by a glacier and called Coggin's Pond.

"Those children, close to middle age now and with children of their own, have not had to learn the hard way that the harbor and the marsh and the pond are for them as portable as their souls. Their childhood home in Barnstable is still in the family. They own it jointly now. Their mother left it to them, along with the royalties from her book, if any, in her simple will. One of them, a painter, lives there all year round with her husband and their son. The other heirs visit it frequently with their mates and children, and especially in the good old summertime.

"Their own children, whether by the harbor or the pond or the marsh, which has patches of quicksand, are themselves learning how to get safely home before the sun goes down. They are so numerous! They are monolingual and of mixed ancestry, and no doubt have several words in common which will never appear in any dictionary, since they themselves invented them.

"And here is almost the last word in *The Brothers Karamazov*: 'Hurrah!' "

(That piece, too, was published by *Architectural Digest*. I like to write for it because my father and his father were architects. My appearing in a journal celebrating their profession may be a reproach, a way of saying to their ghosts that if only Father had encouraged me, I could have been and should have been the next in a long line of Indiana architects named Vonnegut. There is in fact a young architect named Scott Vonnegut working in Vermont now, the son of my big brother Bernard. But Vermont is nothing like Indiana, and Scott is not and cannot be what I might have been, which is a partner of my father.)

V

I never met my architect grandfather Bernard, but I have been told that he so disliked his native Indianapolis that he was relieved to die there when he was still fairly young. He would have preferred to live in New York City or Europe, where he had spent much of his youth and early manhood. My guess is that he would have been bemused by his barbarous Hoosier grandchildren, always yearning to be elsewhere—in beautiful Dresden on the Elbe, perhaps.

My father, as I have said elsewhere ad nauseam, said I could go to college only if I studied chemistry. How flattered I would have been if he had said instead that I, too, should become an architect.

(My goodness! What a lot of heavy psychological stevedoring I have done so early on! Already I have explained why I am secretly frightened of women and why I wear a shit-eating grin every time the subject of conversation is architecture.)

At a memorial service for the brilliant author Donald Barthelme (who was surely sorry to die, since he was going from strength to strength), I said off the cuff that we had had a secret bond, as though we were both descended from Estonians, say, or Frisian Islanders. (This would have been in November 1989.) Barthelme and I had known each other for many years but were not particularly close. Often when our eyes met, though, there flashed between us an acknowledgment of the secret bond and its complex implications.

This was it: We were the sons of architects.

This explained why we were aggressively unconventional storytellers, even though we knew that literary conventions were a form of politeness to readers, and on no grounds to be despised. (Literature, unlike any other art form, requires those who enjoy it to be performers. Reading is a performance, and anything a writer can do to make this difficult activity easier is of benefit to all concerned. Why write a symphony, so to speak, which can't even be played by the New York Philharmonic?) As sons of architects, though, Barthelme and I tried hard to make every architect's dream come true, which is a dwelling such as no one has ever seen before, but which proves to be eminently inhabitable.

Casualties have been heavy among American writers I have cared a lot about. (Actuaries for life insurance companies would be unsurprised by such an announcement by a man sixty-seven years of age.) There was a memorial service for Bernard Malamud, dead at seventy-one, four days after Barthelme's. (I missed it. I was sick. If I had been there, I would have read aloud from his own work.) My Long Island summer neighbors James Jones and Nelson Algren and Truman Capote and Irwin Shaw have all been augered in. Barthelme was the youngest and the least used-up to be forced to leave. He was only fifty-eight. (The average age of a killed American in World War II was twenty-six. In Vietnam it was twenty. What a shame! What a shame!)

Nelson Algren lived to be seventy-two (as did my father). I said this about him in an introduction for a new edition of his

Never Come Morning (Four Walls Eight Windows, 1987): "According to the diary of my wife Jill Krementz, the young British-Indian novelist Salman Rushdie came to our house in Sagaponack, Long Island, for lunch on May 9, 1981. His excellent novel *Midnight's Children* had just been published in the United States, and he told us that the most intelligent review had been written by Nelson Algren, a man he would like to meet. I replied that we knew Algren some, since Jill had photographed him several times and he and I had been teachers at the Writers' Workshop of the University of Iowa back in 1965, when we were both dead broke and I was forty-three and he was fifty-six.

"I said, too, that Algren was one of the few writers I knew who was really funny in conversations. I offered as a sample what Algren had said at the Workshop after I introduced him to the Chilean novelist José Donoso: 'I think it would be nice to come from a country that long and narrow.'

"Rushdie was really in luck, I went on, because Algren lived only a few miles to the north, in Sag Harbor, where John Steinbeck had spent the last of his days, and he was giving a cocktail party that very afternoon. I would call him and tell him we were bringing Rushdie along, and Jill would take pictures of the two of them together, both writers about people who were very poor. I suggested that the party might be the only one that Algren had given for himself in his entire life, since, no matter how famous he became, he remained a poor man living among the poor, and usually alone. He was living alone in Sag Harbor. He had had a new wife in Iowa City, but that marriage lived about as long as a soap bubble. His enthusiasm for writing, reading, and gambling left little time for the duties of a married man.

"I said that Algren was bitter about how little he had been paid over the years for such important work, and especially for the movie rights to what may be his masterpiece, *The Man with the Golden Arm*, which made a huge amount of money as a Frank Sinatra film. Not a scrap of the profits had come to Algren, and I heard him say one time, 'I am the penny whistle of American literature.'

"When we got up from lunch, I went to the phone and dialed Algren's number. A man answered and said, 'Sag Harbor Police Department.'

" 'Sorry,' I said. 'Wrong number.'

" 'Who were you calling?' he said.

" 'Nelson Algren,' I said.

" 'This is his house,' he said, 'but Mr. Algren is dead.' A heart attack that morning had killed Algren.

"He is buried in Sag Harbor—without a widow or descendants, hundreds and hundreds of miles from Chicago, Illinois, which had given him to the world and with whose underbelly he had been so long identified. Like James Joyce, he had become an exile from his homeland after writing that his neighbors were perhaps not as noble and intelligent and kindly as they liked to think they were.

"Only a few weeks before his death, he had been elected by his supposed peers, myself among them, to membership in the American Academy and Institute of Arts and Letters—a certification of respectability withheld from many wonderful writers, incidentally, including James Jones and Irwin Shaw. This was surely not the first significant honor ever accorded him. When he was at the peak of his powers and fame in the middle of this century, he regularly won prizes for short stories and was the first recipient of a National Book Award for Fiction, and so on. And only a few years before his death the American Academy and Institute had given him its Medal for Literature, without, however, making him a member. Among the few persons to win this medal were the likes of William Faulkner and Ernest Hemingway.

"His response to the medal had been impudent. He was still living in Chicago, and I myself talked to him on the telephone, begging him to come to New York City to get it at a big ceremony, with all expenses paid. His final statement on the subject to me was this: 'I'm sorry, but I have to speak at a ladies' garden club that day.'

"At the cocktail party whose prospect may have killed him, I had hoped to ask him if membership in the American Academy and Institute had pleased him more than the medal. Other friends of his have since told me that the membership had moved him tremendously and had probably given him the nerve to throw a party. As to how the seeming insult of a medal without a membership had ever taken shape: This was nothing but a clumsy clerical accident caused by the awarders of prizes and memberships, writers as lazy and absentminded and idiosyncratic in such matters as Algren himself.

"God knows *how* it happened. But all's well that ends well, as the poet said.

"Another thing I heard from others, but never from Algren himself, was how much he hoped to be remembered after he was gone. It was always women who spoke so warmly of this. If it turned out that he had never mentioned the possibility of his own immortality to any man, that would seem in character. When *I* saw him with men, he behaved as though he wanted nothing more from life than a night at the fights, a day at the track, or a table-stakes poker game. This was a pose, of course, and perceived as such by one and all. It was also perceived back in Iowa City that he was a steady and heavy loser at gambling, and that his writing was not going well. He had already produced so *much,* most of it in the mood of the Great Depression, which had become ancient history. He appeared to want to modernize himself somehow. What was my evidence? There he was, a master storyteller, blasted beyond all reason with admiration for and envy of a moderately innovative crime story then appearing in serial form in *The New Yorker,* Truman Capote's *In Cold Blood.* For a while in Iowa, he could talk of little else.

"While he was only thirteen years my senior, so close to my own age that we were enlisted men in Europe in the same world war, he was a pioneering ancestor of mine in the compressed history of American literature. He broke new ground by depicting persons said to be dehumanized by poverty and ignorance and injustice as being *genuinely* dehumanized, and dehumanized quite *permanently*. Contrast, as if you will, the poor people in Algren's tales with those in the works of social reformers such as Charles Dickens and George Bernard Shaw, and particularly with those in Shaw's *Pygmalion,* with their very promising wit and resourcefulness and courage. Reporting on what he saw of dehumanized Americans with his own eyes day after day, year after year, Algren said in effect, 'Hey—an awful lot of these people your hearts are bleeding for are really mean and stupid. That's just a fact. Did you know that?'

"And why didn't he soften his stories, as most writers would have, with characters with a little wisdom and power who did all they could to help the dehumanized? His penchant for truth again shoved him in the direction of unpopularity. Altruists in his experience were about as common as unicorns, and especially in Chicago, which he once described to me as 'the only major city in the country where you can easily buy your way out of a murder rap.'

"So—was there anything he expected to accomplish with so much dismaying truthfulness? He gives the answer himself, I think, in his preface to this book. As I understand him, he would be satisfied were we to agree with him that persons unlucky and poor and not very bright are to be respected for surviving, although they often have no choice but to do so in ways unattractive and blameworthy to those who are a lot better off.

"It seems to me now that Algren's pessimism about so much of earthly life was Christian. Like Christ, as we know Him from the Bible, he was enchanted by the hopeless, could not take his eyes off them, and could see little good news for them in the future, given what they had become and what Caesar was like and so on, unless beyond death there awaited something more humane."

My introduction stops here. I knew very little about Algren's sex life (or about my own, for that matter). I subsequently learned from Deirdre Bair's *Simone de Beauvoir* (Summit, 1990) that he helped Miss de Beauvoir achieve her first orgasm. (The only person I ever helped achieve a first orgasm was good old me.) In Iowa City, Algren would refer to her as "Madame Yak Yak" because she had given their relationship so much publicity.

I wrote an introduction to a collection of short stories by Budd Schulberg, too, and a long salutation for a Festschrift presented to Erskine Caldwell on his eightieth birthday. (He still had three years to go.) I have misplaced copies of both, which is probably just as well. In both, I remember, I exclaimed over the foreshortening of American literary history, in which seeming generations of writers may be separated by less than twenty years. When I set out to be a professional writer of fiction, Irwin Shaw and Nelson Algren and William Saroyan and John Cheever and Erskine Caldwell and Budd Schulberg and James T. Farrell seemed as ancestral as Mark Twain or Nathaniel Hawthorne. But I would come to be friends with all of them. And why not? With the exception of Caldwell, most were about the age of my big brother, Bernard. (I never met John Steinbeck, but I know his widow, Elaine, and she is about my late sister's age.)

It is the spectacular violence modern times wreak on culture which accounts for this foreshortening, surely. We are defined by booms and busts, and by wars radically different in mood and purpose and technology. My wife, Jill, covered the Vietnam War as a photographer. To the young people she now does books about, that war might as well have been a thousand years ago.

Yes, and to me as a schoolboy during the Great Depression, which defined Steinbeck and Saroyan and Algren, World War I, which defined Ernest Hemingway, might also have been a thousand years ago, but I knew his widow, Mary, too, and he was born after (but died sooner than) my Uncle Alex, who went to Harvard because his big brother was at MIT.

"I did not know Ernest Hemingway," I told a group of Hemingway scholars convening in Boise, Idaho, a couple of years ago. "He was twenty-three years my senior. He would now be ninety. We were born in the Middle West, we set out to be reporters, our fathers were gun nuts, we felt profoundly indebted to Mark Twain, and we were the children of suicides.

"I am not aware that he thought much about my own generation of American novelists. Norman Mailer, I know, sent him a copy of *The Naked and the Dead,* soon after it was published. The package was returned unopened. Hemingway chided Irwin Shaw for having, as he put it, dared to go into the ring with Tolstoy by writing a novel which viewed a war from both sides of the battle lines, *The Young Lions.* I know of only two members of my generation he praised: Nelson Algren, the Chicago tough guy and friend of boxers and gamblers, and Vance Bourjaily, the hunting enthusiast who was in World War II what Hemingway had been in the first one, a civilian ambulance driver attached to a combat unit.

"James Jones, author of *From Here to Eternity,* and a rifleman in peacetime and then in war, told me that he could not consider Hemingway a fellow soldier, since he had never submitted to training and discipline. In the Spanish Civil War and then in World War II, Hemingway took no orders and gave no orders. He came and went wherever and whenever he pleased. He actually hunted German submarines for a while in the Caribbean—in his own boat and of his own accord.

"He was a reporter of war, and one of the best the world has ever known. So was Tolstoy—who was in addition a real soldier.

"During World War I, the United States got into the fighting so late that an American with true war stories to tell, and a wound besides, was something of a rarity. Such was Hemingway's situation. He was an even rarer sort of American, again fresh from a battlefield, when he wrote about the Spanish Civil War during the 1930s.

"But then the coinage of true battle stories by Americans was utterly debased by World War II, when millions upon millions of us fought overseas and came home no longer needing a Hemingway to say what war was like. Joseph Heller told me he would have been in the dry-cleaning business now, if it weren't for World War II.

"Heller is, of course, the author of *Catch-22*, a far more influential book nowadays than *A Farewell to Arms* or *For Whom the Bell Tolls*. The key word in this speech is 'nowadays.'

"Hemingway was unquestionably an artist of the first rank, with an admirable soul, the size of Kilimanjaro. His choice of subject matter, though, bullfighting and nearly forgotten wars and shooting big animals for sport, often makes him a little hard to read nowadays. Conservation and humane treatment of animals and contempt for the so-called arts of war rank high on most of our agendas nowadays.

"How many of us can find pleasure nowadays in these words from Hemingway's *Green Hills of Africa*, reportage, not fiction, describing a lion hunt fifty-three years ago: 'I knew that if I could kill one alone . . . I would feel good about it for a long time. I had in my mind absolutely not to shoot unless I knew I could kill him. I had killed three and knew what it consisted in, but I was getting more excitement from this one than the whole trip.' Imagine boasting of killing three lions, and reporting delight at the prospect of killing a fourth one, nowadays.

"Vance Bourjaily, admired, as I've said, by Hemingway, gave me a rule of thumb about hunting. 'The bigger the game,' he said, 'the more corrupted the soul of the hunter.' As for the glamour of big game hunting nowadays: It is predicted that the last East African elephant will die of starvation or be killed for its ivory in about eight years.

"As for bullfighting: It is an enterprise so little admired in this country by most people that it is in fact against the law. I don't have to say 'nowadays.' Bullfighting was against the law here long before the birth of Hemingway. Paradoxically, I find his bullfighting stories among my favorites still. That could be because they are so alien to my own passions and experiences that I can accept them as ethnography, as accounts by an explorer of a society for which I bear no responsibility.

"Let me hasten to say that no matter how much his choice of subject matter bothers me nowadays, I am always amazed and delighted by the power he discovered in the simplest language. A sample I choose at random from his short story 'Big Two-Hearted River': 'Nick sat down against the charred stump and smoked a cigarette. His pack balanced on the top of the stump, harness holding ready, a hollow molded in it from his back. Nick sat smoking, looking out over the country. He did not need to get his map out. He knew where he was from the position of the river.

" 'As he smoked, his legs stretched out in front of him, he noticed a grasshopper walk along the ground and up onto his woolen sock. The grasshopper was black. As he had walked along the road, climbing, he had started many grasshoppers from the dust. They were all black.'

"(The grasshoppers were black, of course, because the area had been burned over recently, making black the ideal protective coloration.)

"No fear of repeating words there. How many of you had teachers who told you never to use the same word twice in a paragraph, or even in adjacent paragraphs? Clearly, that was poor advice. The biggest word in that passage, by the way, is 'grasshopper.' Big enough! The strongest word is 'black.' Strong enough!

"I myself, when I teach writing, say that people will not read a story in which nothing much happens. But nothing much happens in two of Hemingway's most thrilling stories, 'A Clean, Well-Lighted Place' and, again, 'Big Two-Hearted River.' How is this possible? It is the brushwork. If Hemingway had been a painter, I would say of him that while I often don't like the subjects he celebrates, I sure as heck respect his brushwork.

"Ah me! He is what we call 'dated' now. Yes, and we can all expect in this volatile century to find enthusiasms and passions of our years as young adults to become dated, too. What happened to Hemingway has happened or will happen to all of us, writers or not. It can't be helped, so no person should be scorned when it happens to her or him. The sharks almost always get the big marlins, the big truths we reel in so proudly when we are young.

"I have named one of the sharks which took a bite out of Hemingway's marlin: the conservation movement. Another one is feminism. I don't think I need expand on that. It must be plain to everyone that the Ladies' Auxiliary for Men Engaged in Blood Sports has been disbanded for quite some time.

"Ernest Hemingway is still quite famous, although he is not taught much anymore in colleges and universities. When all is said and done, it is teachers who keep literary reputations alive or let them fade away. For a while there, Hemingway was as imposing as General Motors or The New York Times. Think of that: One human being somehow becoming as majestic as major institutions. Think of Harriet Beecher Stowe. Such is the power sometimes of printed words.

"We have seen the power demonstrated again very recently and tragically. I refer to the case of Salman Rushdie, who unwittingly made himself with one book the world's second most famous Moslem and caused an entire nation to declare war to the death on him.

"A couple of decades ago a lonely novelist embarrassed the Soviet Union as profoundly as would have a great military defeat. I speak of Aleksandr Solzhenitsyn. But I digress. Stowe's and Solzhenitsyn's and poor Salman Rushdie's importance in the eyes of the world rests in large part on their willingness to oppose certain easily identifiable factions in society. Hemingway

seemed just as important for a while without arousing any enemies, without calling for any sort of reforms. His antifascism,
on paper anyway, was of an unanalytical, rosy-cheeked-school-
boy variety.

"So whence came the power which made him for a little while
as respected as Stowe or Solzhenitsyn or poor Rushdie—or
General Motors or *The New York Times*? I suggest to you that
it inhered in his celebration of male bonding at a time when
there was a widespread dread here and in Europe of seeming
homosexual.

"The great anthropologist Margaret Mead was asked one
time, and she had studied men, women, and children in every
sort of society, when it was that men were happiest. She thought
awhile, and then she said, 'When they're starting out on a hunt
with no women or children along.' I think she was right. Don't
you? Back when war was another sort of hunt, going on the
warpath must have induced the same sort of happiness. I will
guess further that permission for males to bond with one another, which was given to such an expedition by the women
and children, was a principal ingredient of that happiness.

"I am not talking about clinical homosexuality. I am perfectly
willing to do so, but at another time. When I assert that male
bonding, one man's feeling love for another one in the neighborhood of danger, is often the greatest reward for a character
in a story by Ernest Hemingway, I am not saying that Ernest
Hemingway was gay. He was not gay, and you don't have to
take my word for it. You can ask Marlene Dietrich, who is still
alive and as beautiful as ever. What legs!

"The last time I was in Boise, also as a lecturer, I met a nice
woman with a wry sense of humor about men. Her husband
was then out hunting with heavy-duty equipment and pals. She
laughed about that. She said men had to get out of doors and
drink and kill things before they could show how much they
loved each other. She thought it was ridiculous that they had
to go to so much trouble and expense before they could express

something as simple and natural as love. Which reminds me of what Vance Bourjaily said to me about duck hunting. He said it was like standing in a cold shower with all your clothes on and tearing up twenty-dollar bills.

"May I say parenthetically that I myself was once a rifleman in time of war and experienced on occasion that kind of love Hemingway so enjoyed. It can be terrific.

"And enough of that. I'm embarrassed.

"Few writers in midlife have as clear an idea as Hemingway did of what, God willing, they have yet to accomplish. I sure didn't. I sure don't. When he was thirty-nine years old, with, as it turned out, twenty-three more years to go, he said that he hoped to write three more novels and twenty-five more stories. He had by then published all of the forty-nine superb stories which nowadays appear to be his most durable contributions to literature. He would not give us twenty-five more. He wouldn't give us even one more.

"He had by then published four novels: *The Torrents of Spring, The Sun Also Rises,* which made him a world figure, *A Farewell to Arms,* which confirmed his planetary importance, and *To Have and Have Not,* a much weaker book. He would honor the contract he made with himself in 1938 by actually delivering three more novels: *For Whom the Bell Tolls, Across the River and into the Trees,* and the short book which won him a deserved Nobel Prize, *The Old Man and the Sea.*

"That last one, of course, is about what sharks did to an old man's marlin. In terms of ordinary life expectancy Hemingway wasn't an old man when he wrote it, but he obviously felt like one.

"Seven years of literary silence followed his acceptance of the 1954 Nobel Prize. And then, not far from here, he created what he may have considered yet another work of art, although a most horrible one, his self-inflicted death by gunshot. It seems likely to me that he believed his life to be the most memorable of all his stories, in which case that gunshot was a form of typography, a period. 'The end.'

"I am reminded of the suicide of another American genius, George Eastman, inventor of the Kodak camera and roll film, and founder of the Eastman Kodak Company. He shot himself in 1932. Eastman, who was not ill and was not suffering from grief, said in his suicide note what Ernest Hemingway must have felt when he was close to the end: 'My work is done.'

"I thank you for your attention."

(After that speech, a bunch of us were loaded onto a yellow school bus and taken to a Spanish restaurant.)

Hemingway was a member of what is now called the American Academy and Institute of Arts and Letters. Founded in 1898, it presently has an upper and a lower house, the much smaller Academy being the commissioned officers, so to speak, and the Institute being enlisted personnel. (I myself am a PFC, and it may be that my dossier from ROTC at Cornell still follows me.) Truman Capote made it into the upper house. So did Erskine Caldwell. Nelson Algren made it into the lower house by the hair of his chinny-chin-chin. James Jones and Irwin Shaw died outsiders, somehow lacking that certain something our organization was looking for.

(I said of Jones, in a blurb for *The James Jones Reader* [Birch Lane Press, 1991], that he was the Tolstoy of American foot soldiers in the last just war, in the now vanished Age of the Common Man. He was that common man, but also a genius. I meant it.)

It is a random matter who gets in and who doesn't, since it is loonies who do the nominating and then the voting, which is to say the artists and writers and musicians who already belong. They are no good at what is primarily office work, are notoriously absentminded, are commonly either ignorant or envious of good work others may be doing, and so on. There is also a lot of logrolling, with writers saying to painters and musicians in effect, "I'll vote for somebody I never heard of in your field, if you'll vote for somebody you never heard of in mine." And so on.

Sometimes I think the American Academy and Institute of Arts and Letters shouldn't exist, since it has the power not only to honor but to insult. Look what it did to James Jones and Irwin Shaw. They couldn't help feeling like something the cat drug in whenever the Academy and Institute was mentioned. There are surely more than one hundred living American creative people of the highest excellence who feel that way this very day.

The great Hoosier humorist Kin Hubbard (never considered for membership) said that it was no disgrace to be poor, but that it might as well be. It is also no disgrace to be excluded by the Academy and Institute. But it might as well be.

Tennessee Williams (1911–1983) *was* a member, thank goodness. (After all, he was our most excellent playwright.) Before Jill and I lived together, she brought him around to my apartment one night. I was so excited to meet a person who wrote that troublingly and amusingly and sympathetically about Americans who didn't live in New York City that I bloodied my shins on my marble coffee table, trying to get to him so I could shake his hand. (He and T. S. Eliot grew up in St. Louis, but Williams admitted it. He didn't all of a sudden start talking like the Archbishop of Canterbury.)

The only thing I ever wrote about him, though, was a note I hand-delivered to the actress Maria Tucci, who lives across the street. She was in rehearsal for Williams's *The Night of the Iguana* and had told me that the cast members weren't as comfortable with the play as they would like to be. My note said that an iguana was disgusting to look at but was in fact good to eat. The message I got from the play, I went on, was that it was better to love something other people might think was ugly than not to love at all. Eat an iguana, and you could wind up as well nourished as anyone.

VI

(Trivia: Aldous Huxley died on the same day as John F. Kennedy. Louis-Ferdinand Céline died two days after Ernest Hemingway.)

A requiem is a mass for the dead, customarily sung in Latin. To those who know little Latin, which is my case, its words are nonsensically beautiful. Who cares what they mean? A mass which many composers have set to music was promulgated by Pope St. Pius V in 1570, by decree of the Council of Trent. The year of its promulgation is much, much closer to our own time than to that of Jesus Christ.

It begins and ends unobjectionably enough, *"Requiem aeternam dona eis, Domine; et lux perpetua luceat eis,"* which means in English, "Rest eternal grant them, O Lord, and let light perpetual shine upon them." (A credulous and literal-minded person might conclude from this that Huxley and Kennedy and Céline and Hemingway and my sister and my first wife Jane and all the rest of the dead are now trying to get some sleep with the lights on.)

On February 12, 1985, my second wife Jill and I attended the world premiere of a new musical setting for this mass composed by Andrew Lloyd Webber (born in 1948, at which time I was a public-relations man for General Electric). Lloyd Webber by then had already composed the music for *Jesus Christ Superstar, Evita,* and *Cats.* (T. S. Eliot, whose poems about cats inspired that last-named musical, owed an unacknowledged debt, it has always seemed to me, to *Archie and Mehitabel* by Don Marquis, whose wife was the former Mrs. Walter Vonnegut.)

The premiere of Lloyd Webber's requiem took place in St. Thomas Church on Fifth Avenue in Manhattan, an outspokenly Anglican institution, although the specifically Roman Catholic words (lyrics) of the mass drew much of their anger from the fact of England's having denied the spiritual supremacy of the Papacy. If I am any judge, the black-tie audience was about half Protestant and half Jewish. (Some of the musicians and TV cameramen and policemen outside were probably Catholics.)

Nobody seemed to know or care what the Latin words meant or where they came from. We were all there for the music. (Or maybe because that was the chic place to be that night.) After all, Placido Domingo (one of the Catholic musicians) was going to do a lot of the singing, along with the combined boys' choirs of St. Thomas Church and Winchester Cathedral (all the way from England), backed up by members of the New York Philharmonic. Off they went, *"Requiem aeternam dona eis, Domine,"* et cetera. I was beguiled by the cat face and silvery voice of the soloist of the Winchester Boys' Choir, and looked into my program to learn his name. God love him, he was Paul Miles-Kingston.

But then something else in the program caught my eye, which was a translation into English of the words of the mass, the last things anybody there gave a darn about. They were terrible! (And lest somebody think I am mocking Holy Scripture, I point out again that the mass was as frankly manmade and as nearly contemporary, taking the long view of history, as Hemingway's *Green Hills of Africa*.)

Domingo and Paul Miles-Kingston and Lloyd Webber's soprano wife Sarah Brightman and all the rest of them onstage, in front of the organ pipes, were behaving as though God were a wonderful person who had prepared all sorts of goodies which we could enjoy after we were dead. They were in fact, if only they had known what they were saying, promising a Paradise indistinguishable from the Spanish Inquisition.

"Quantus tremor est futurus, quando judex est venturus, cuncta stricte discussurus!" Whoopee! What fun! How nice. Except that what that means is, "What trembling there will be when the Judge shall come to examine everything in strict justice!"

"Quid sum miser tunc dicturus? Quem patronum rogaturus, cum vix justus sit securus?" From the performers' expressions and body language you would have concluded that the weak wouldn't have to be afraid in Heaven, that they would find kindness and forgiveness on all sides. You would have been badly mistaken. The performers were singing, "What shall I, a wretch, say at that time? What advocate shall I entreat to plead for me when scarcely the righteous shall be safe from damnation?"

Ain't that nice? ("Get a lawyer," says the mass.)

Nearly the entire mass was that sadistic and masochistic. (You can find how it goes, from start to finish, in the Appendix. Decide for yourself.) So after Jill and I got home, I stayed up half the night writing a better one. (That is not a vain statement. Anybody could write a better one and nobody could write a worse one.) I got rid of the judges and the tortures and the lions' mouths, and having to sleep with the lights on. (I have tossed that into the Appendix, too, so again, decide for yourself.)

I did not think it was very good poetry, and so I was eager (as were the lyricists at the Council of Trent, no doubt) to get it put into Latin as quickly as possible. As I told my wife, I wanted to find somebody who could put it through the hocus-pocus laundromat. I was willing to pay good money.

I tried Fordham first, but was turned down there on the grounds of heresy. But then I found a specialist in Church Latin at New York University, John F. Collins, who agreed to be my hired gun, come hell or high water. Like Placido Domingo, he is a Catholic. "Rest eternal grant them, O Cosmos, and let not light disturb their sleep," my mass began. After John Collins put it through the hocus-pocus laundromat, it came out like this: "*Requiem aeternam dona eis, Munde, neve lux somnum perturbet eorum.*"

I was called for jury duty soon thereafter. There I met a composer named Edgar Grana, a Juilliard graduate who had been a student at the University of Iowa when I was a teacher there back in 1965. (One of my former students there, John Casey, won the 1989 National Book Award for Fiction, which is more than I ever did.) Grana spent the next year setting Collins's Latin to music at his own expense. We shopped it around several churches here in New York without any luck. (I would say the music was sort of a postmodern, multiple-crossover, semiclassical bebop lemon marmalade.)

But then Barbara Wagner, the director of the best Unitarian Universalist choir in the country (lots of ringers), which is in Buffalo, said she wanted to do it. She started rehearsals right after Christmas, and by golly if we didn't have our own world premiere on March 13, 1988, in her church. That was a Sunday night. I had lectured for money the night before in the same space, in order to pay for four synthesizer virtuosi. They were the orchestra.

I was so excited that my hair stood on end during the ten seconds of perfect silence before the first note was played.

When it was all over, though, I hadn't heard a single word distinctly. That is how overwhelming the music was. (Mark Twain said of Italian opera that he hadn't heard anything like it since the orphanage burned down.) So that was that. The composer and the performers had a stunning success, with a standing ovation and flowers and all the rest of it. I alone was disappointed, a crank who cared about the language.

That is pretty much the end of the story about my requiem, premiered three years after Andrew Lloyd Webber's, except that my wife Jill subsequently ran into Lloyd Webber in London. She said to him, "My husband also wrote a requiem."

He replied, as though he had started a fad, "Oh, I know. Now everybody is writing requiems."

He missed the point I had tried to make by writing new language rather than new music for a mass for the dead: In the beginning was the word.

(Speaking of composers: My sister Alice asked our father when she was about ten years old if he and Mother used to dance to Beethoven.)

VII

And speaking of revered old documents which cry out for a rewrite nowadays, how about the First Amendment to the Constitution of the United States of America, which reads:

"Congress shall make no law respecting an establishment of religion, or prohibiting the free exercise thereof; or abridging the freedom of speech, or of the press; or the right of the people peaceably to assemble, and to petition the Government for a redress of grievances." What we have there is what should have been at least three separate amendments, and maybe as many as five, hooked together willy-nilly in one big Dr. Seuss animal of a nonstop sentence. It is as though a starving person, rescued at last, blurted out all the things he or she had dreamed of eating while staying barely alive on bread and water.

When James Madison put together the first ten Amendments, the "Bill of Rights," in 1778, there was so much blurting by male property owners ravenous for liberty that he had 210 proposed limitations on the powers of the Government to choose from. (In my opinion, the thing most well-fed people want above all else from their Government is, figuratively speaking, the right to shoot craps with loaded dice. They wouldn't get that until President Ronald Reagan.)

I said to a lawyer for the American Civil Liberties Union that Madison's First Amendment wasn't as well written as it might have been.

"Maybe he didn't expect us to take him so seriously," he said.

I think there is a chance of that, although the lawyer was being wryly jocular. So far as I know, Madison did not laugh or otherwise demur when Thomas Jefferson (who owned slaves) called the Constitutional Convention in Philadelphia an assembly of demi-Gods. People two-thirds of the way to the top of Mount Olympus might not take as seriously as some of us do the possibility of actually honoring among the squabbling mortals the airy, semi-divine promises of the Bill of Rights.

The ACLU lawyer said that I, as a writer, should admire Madison for making his Amendments as unambiguous as a light switch, which can be only "on" or "off," by the strong use of absolute negatives: "Congress shall make *no* law . . . shall *not* be infringed . . . No soldier shall . . . shall *not* be violated, and *no* warrants shall issue. . . . No person shall be held to answer . . . *no* fact tried by a jury . . . shall *not* be required . . . shall *not* be construed. . . ." There are no words anywhere in his Amendments meaning "under ideal conditions" or "whenever possible" or "at the convenience of the Government." From moment to moment in our now long history (the oldest continuous government save for Switzerland's), the several specific provisions of the Bill of Rights can be, thanks to James Madison, only "off" or "on."

To me the First Amendment sounds more like a dream than a statute. The right to say or publish absolutely anything makes me feel as insubstantial as a character in somebody else's dream when I defend it, as I often do. It is such a *tragic* freedom since there is no limit to the vileness some people are proud to express in public if allowed to do so with impunity. So again and again in debates with representatives of the Moral Majority and the like, and some of the angrier Women Against Pornography, I find myself charged with being an encourager of violence against women and kiddie porn.

When I was new at such discussions I insouciantly asked a fundamentalist Christian opponent ("Oh, come on now, Reverend") if he knew of anyone who had been ruined by a book. (Mark Twain claimed to have been ruined by salacious parts of the Bible.)

The Reverend was glad I asked. He said that a man out in Oregon had read a pornographic book and then raped a teenage maiden on her way home from the grocery store, and then mutilated her with a broken Coke bottle. (I am sure it really happened.) We were there to discuss the efforts of some parents to get certain books eliminated from school libraries and curricula on the grounds that they were offensive or morally harmful—quite mild and honorable books in any case. But my dumb question gave the Reverend the opportunity to link the books in question to the most hideous sexual crimes.

The books he and his supporters wanted out of the schools, one of mine among them, were not pornographic, although he would have liked our audience to think so. (There *is* the word "motherfucker" one time in my *Slaughterhouse-Five*, as in "Get out of the road, you dumb motherfucker." Ever since that word was published, way back in 1969, children have been attempting to have intercourse with their mothers. When it will stop no one knows.) The fault of *Slaughterhouse-Five*, James Dickey's *Deliverance*, J. D. Salinger's *Catcher in the Rye*, several books by Judy Blume, and so on, as far as the Reverend was concerned, was that neither their authors nor their characters exemplified his notion of ideal Christian behavior and attitudes.

The Reverend (as was his right) was making an undisguised attack not only on Americans' demi-God–given right to consider every sort of idea (including his), but also on the Constitution's insistence that the Government (including the public schools) not declare one religion superior to any other and behave accordingly with the force of law.

So the Reverend was not a hypocrite. He was perfectly willing to say in so many words that there was nothing sacred about the First Amendment, and that many images and ideas other than pornography should be taken out of circulation by the police, and that the official religion of the whole country should be his sort of Christianity. He was sincere in believing that my *Slaughterhouse-Five* might somehow cause a person to wind up in a furnace for all eternity (see the mass promulgated by Pope St. Pius V), which would be even worse (if you consider its duration) than being raped, murdered, and then mutilated by a man maddened by dirty pictures.

He in fact won my sympathy (easy to do). He was not a television evangelist (so easily and justly caricatured), although he probably preached on radio from time to time. (They all do.) He was a profoundly sincere Christian and family man, doing a pretty good job no doubt of imitating the life of Christ as he understood it, sexually clean, and not pathologically fond of the goods of this Earth and so on. He was trying to hold together an extended family, a support system far more dependable than anything the Government could put together, in sickness as in health, for richer or for poorer, whose bond was commonly held beliefs and attitudes. (I had studied anthropology, after all, and so knew in my bones that human beings can't like life very much if they don't belong to a clan associated with a specific piece of real estate.)

The Attorney General's Commission on Pornography, a traveling show about dirty books and pictures put on the road during the administration of Ronald Reagan, was something else again. At least a couple of the panel members would later be revealed as having been in the muck of financial or sexual atrocities. There was a clan feeling, to be sure, but the family property in this case was the White House, and an amiable, sleepy, absentminded old movie actor was its totem pole. And the crazy quilt of ideas all its members had to profess put the Council of Trent to shame for mean-spirited, objectively batty fantasias: that it was good that civilians could buy assault rifles; that the contras in Nicaragua were a lot like Thomas Jefferson and James Madison; that Palestinians were to be called "terrorists" at every opportunity; that the contents of wombs were Government property; that the American Civil Liberties Union was a subversive organization; that anything that sounded like the Sermon on the Mount was socialist or communist, and therefore anti-American; that people with AIDS, except for those who got it from mousetrapped blood transfusions, had asked for it; that a billion-dollar airplane was well worth the price; and on and on.

The Attorney General's Commission on Pornography was blatantly show business, a way for the White House to draw attention to its piety by means of headlines about sex, and to imply yet again that those in favor of freedom of speech were enthusiasts for sexual exploitation of children and rape and so on. (While other Reagan supporters were making private the funds for public housing and cleaning out the savings banks.)

So I asked to appear before the Commission when it came to New York, but my offer was declined. I wanted to say, "I have read much of the heartrending testimony about the damage words and pictures can do which has been heard by your committee. The scales have fallen from my eyes. I now understand that our Government must have the power to suppress words and images which are causes of sexually motivated insanity and crimes. As John the Apostle says, 'In the beginning was the word.'

"I make my living with words, and I am ashamed. In view of the damage freely circulated ideas can do to a society, and particularly to children, I beg my Government to delete from my works all thoughts which might be dangerous. Save me from myself. I beg for the help of our elected leaders in bringing my thoughts into harmony with their own and those of the people who elected them. That is democracy.

"Attempting to make amends at this late date, I call the attention of this committee, and God bless the righteous Edwin Meese, to the fundamental piece of obscenity from which all others spring, the taproot of the tree whose fruit is so poisonous. I will read it aloud, so audience members under the age of twenty-one should leave the room. Those over twenty-one who have heart trouble or are prone to commit rape at the drop of a hat might like to go with them. Don't say I haven't warned you.

"You Commission members have no choice but to stay, no matter what sort of filth is turned loose by witnesses. That can't be easy. You must be very brave. I like to think of you as sort of sewer astronauts.

"All right? Stick your fingers in your ears and close your eyes, because here we go:

" 'Congress shall make no law respecting an establishment of religion, or prohibiting the free exercise thereof; or abridging the freedom of speech, or of the press; or the right of the people peaceably to assemble, and to petition the Government for a redress of grievances.' "

End of joke.

(I put together this chapter upon returning home from the burial in Hellertown, Pennsylvania, of an old war buddy named Bernard V. O'Hare. His name will keep popping up as this book goes on. He was a chain-smoking District Attorney for the first half of his career, and then a chain-smoking defense attorney until his death from cancer a little past midnight, June 9, 1990. I asked him when he was still a DA if he was doing much good by putting felons in prison. He said, "No, I think people have more than enough trouble without me piling on." That doesn't have much to do with the First Amendment. It has everything to do with how bereft I am feeling now. I have put into the Appendix what he wrote about our long friendship for a Festschrift Jill gave me on my sixtieth birthday.)

VIII

(The first story of mine which got into trouble with the sincerely Christian far right was about time-travelers who went back to Bible times and discovered that Jesus Christ was five feet, two inches tall. I think I liked Jesus more than the story's naysayers did, since I was asserting that I didn't care how tall or short He was. Bernard V. O'Hare was also short, but not nearly that short, and was still the most effective and humane criminal lawyer in the recent history of Northampton County, Pennsylvania. He was very much a *local* hero. I, his old war buddy, was the only nonfamily mourner from out of state at his funeral.)

The free-speech provisions of the First Amendment guarantee all of us not only benefits but pain. (As the physical fitness experts tell us, "No pain, no gain.") Much of what other Americans say or publish hurts me a lot, makes me want to throw up. Tough luck for me.

When Charlton Heston (a movie actor who once played Jesus with shaved armpits) tells me in TV commercials (public-service announcements?) about all the good work the National Rifle

Association (to which Father and I both belonged when I was a kid) is doing, and how glad I should be that civilians can and do keep military weapons in their homes or vehicles or places of work, I feel exactly as though he were praising the germs of some loathsome disease, since guns in civilian hands, whether accidentally or on purpose, kill so many of us day after day.

(When I graduated from School Number Forty-three in Indianapolis, each member of our class had to make a public promise as to what he or she would try to do when an adult to make the world a better place. I was going to find a cure for some disease. Well—I sure don't need an electron microscope to identify an AK-47 or an Uzi.)

"A well-regulated Militia, being necessary to the security of a free State," sayeth Article II of the Bill of Rights, "the right of the people to keep and bear arms, shall not be infringed." Perfect! I wouldn't change a word of it. I only wish the NRA and its jellyfishy, well-paid supporters in legislatures both State and Federal would be careful to recite the whole of it, and then tell us how a heavily armed man, woman, or child, recruited by no official, led by no official, given no goals by any official, motivated or restrained only by his or her personality and perceptions of what is going on, can be considered a member of a well-regulated militia.

(To cut a Gordian knot here: I think a sick fantasy is at work, of a sort of Armageddon in which the bad people, poor, dark-skinned, illiterate, lazy, and drug-crazed, will one night attack the neat homes of the good white people who have worked hard for all they have, and have in addition given money and time to charity.)

I used to be very good with guns, was maybe the best shot in my company when I was a PFC. But I wouldn't have one of the motherfuckers in my house for anything.

I consider the discharge of firearms a low form of sport. Modern weapons arc as easy to operate as cigarette lighters. Ask any woman who never worked one before, who went to the local gun shop and joined the NRA's idea of a well-regulated militia and then made Swiss cheese out of a faithless lover or mate. Whenever I hear of somebody that he is a good shot, I think to myself, "That is like saying he is a good man with a Zippo or Bic. Some athlete!"

George Bush, like Charlton Heston, is a lifetime member of the NRA. I am even more offended, though, by his failure to take notice of the most beautiful and noble and brilliant and poetical and sacred accomplishment by Americans to date. I am speaking about the exploration of the Solar System by the camera-bearing space probe *Voyager 2.* This gallant bird (so like Noah's dove) showed us all the outer planets and their moons! We no longer had to guess whether there was life on them or not, or whether our descendants might survive on them! (Forget it.) As *Voyager 2* departed the Solar System forever ("My work is done"), sending us dimmer and dimmer pictures of what we were and where we were, did our President invite us to love it and thank it and wish it well? No. He spoke passionately instead of the necessity of an Amendment to the Constitution (Article XXVII?) outlawing irreverent treatment of a piece of cloth, the American flag. Such an Amendment would be on a nutty par with the Roman Emperor Caligula's having his horse declared a Consul.

(I worry a lot about what they teach at Yale.)

I was able nonetheless to deliver an optimistic graduation address to the Class of 1990 at the University of Rhode Island in Kingston in late May. (The University's soon-to-retire President, Edward D. Eddy, had been a colleague of mine on *The Cornell Daily Sun.* That's what I was doing there.) I prefaced my remarks with a comment on graduation speeches by Kin Hubbard, an Indianapolis humorist who wrote a joke a day for newspapers when I was young. He said that he thought it would be better if colleges would spread the really important stuff over four years instead of saving it all up for the very end.

(In my opinion, Kin Hubbard was as witty as Oscar Wilde,

saying things like, "I don't know anybody who would be willing to work for what he's really worth," and "If somebody says it isn't the money, it's the money," and on and on.)

"The title of my speech," I told the Class of 1990, "is 'Do Not Be Cynical About the American Experiment, Since It Has Only Now Begun.' "

I said that I was often asked to speak about censorship, since my book *Slaughterhouse-Five* was so often tossed out of school libraries. (This is because it is on a list of supposedly dangerous books which has been circulating since 1972 or so. No new books are ever added.) "I have received letters from readers in the Soviet Union," I said, "who were told years ago that my books were being burned up over here." (That happened only in Drake, North Dakota.) "I replied to them that censorship is mostly a rural problem," I went on. "The same communities used to burn people when I was a boy. I feel that we are finally getting somewhere.

"It was mostly black people who were being burned. The most extraordinary change in this country since I was a boy is the decline in racism. Believe me, it could very easily be brought back to full strength again by demagogues. As of this very moment anyway we are fairly good at judging people for what they are rather than for how closely they resemble ourselves and our relatives. We are in fact better at doing that than any other country. In most other countries people wouldn't even consider doing that.

"Who brought about this admirable change in our attitudes? The oppressed and denigrated minorities themselves, with guts and great dignity which they coupled with the promises of the Bill of Rights of the Constitution.

"Is censorship on the rise? You would certainly think so, since it has been in the news so much. But I believe it to be a disease which has been around for a long, long time, like Alzheimer's disease, but which has only recently been identified as a disease and treated. What is new isn't censorship but the fact that it is now recognized as being sickening to our pluralistic democracy, and a lot of good people are trying to do something about it.

"The United States of America had human slavery for almost one hundred years before that custom was recognized as a social disease and people began to fight it. Imagine that. Wasn't that a match for Auschwitz? What a beacon of liberty we were to the rest of the world when it was perfectly acceptable here to own other human beings and treat them as we treated cattle. Who told you we were a beacon of liberty from the very beginning? Why would they lie like that?

"Thomas Jefferson owned slaves, and not many people found that odd. It was as though he had an infected growth on the end of his nose the size of a walnut, and everybody thought that was perfectly OK. I mentioned this one time at the University of Virginia, of which Jefferson was not only the founder but the sublime architect. A history professor explained to me afterward that Jefferson could not free his slaves until he and they were very old, because they were mortgaged and he was broke.

"Imagine that! It used to be legal in this beacon of liberty to hock human beings, maybe even a baby. What a shame that when you find yourself short of cash nowadays you can't take the cleaning lady down to the pawnshop anymore along with your saxophone.

"Now then: Boston and Philadelphia both claim to be the cradle of liberty. Which city is correct? Neither one. Liberty is only now being born in the United States. It wasn't born in 1776. Slavery was legal. Even white women were powerless, essentially the property of their father or husband or closest male relative, or maybe a judge or lawyer. Liberty was only *conceived* in Boston or Philadelphia. Boston or Philadelphia was the motel of liberty, so to speak.

"Now then: The gestation period for a 'possum is twelve days. The gestation period for an Indian elephant is twenty-two months. The gestation period for American liberty, friends and neighbors, turns out to be two hundred years and more!

"Only in my own lifetime has there been serious talk of giving women and racial minorities anything like economic, legal, and social equality. Let liberty be born at last, and let its lusty birth cries be heard in Kingston and in every other city and town and village and hamlet in this vast and wealthy nation, not in Jefferson's time but in the time of the youngest people here this afternoon. Somewhere I heard a baby cry. It should cry for joy.

"Hooray for the Class of 1990 and those who helped them make America stronger by becoming educated citizens.

"I thank you for your attention."

IX

(Rhode Island was the first of the Thirteen Colonies to advocate and implement the right of its citizens to worship or not worship however they pleased.)

Jill Krementz is an Episcopalian (although she goes to church rarely) and I am an atheist (or at best a Unitarian who winds up in churches quite a lot). So when we decided to get married in 1979, having lived together for several years, there seemed a smorgasbord of sacred and secular venues in which we might become as one, so to speak. Since we had met during the production of a play of mine, I suggested that the magic spell be cast at what was said to be the actors' church, "The Little Church Around the Corner," which (hey, presto!) was also Episcopalian, down on Twenty-ninth Street, just off Fifth Avenue in Manhattan. The darling church won its quaint name and reputation for liking theater people in the middle of the nineteenth century, when Joseph Jefferson (author and star of *Rip Van Winkle*) asked to be married in a high Anglican church a couple of blocks north of Twenty-ninth and right on Fifth Avenue. He was told politely that actors were known to be more casual morally than members of that particular congregation, so why didn't he "try the little church around the corner." He did.

So then I did, and never have I caught more hell for having been divorced! (The fact that I was connected with the theater won me no sympathy. Neither did the fact that Jill was a lifelong friend of Paul Moore, the Episcopal Bishop of New York.) It was a woman we talked to. She was obviously powerful, but this was before any women had been ordained. She could be a priest now, and my having divorced my first wife was the most unforgivable thing she had ever heard. (When they got around to ordaining women, one of the first would have this improbable name: Tanya Vonnegut. She was the wife of a cousin of mine, and a great beauty and no doubt an inspiring priest.)

We could get married at The Little Church Around the Corner, according to the battle-axe we spoke to, if I joined the church and did penance with church work, which might include teaching Sunday school. So we put on our show at Christ Church United Methodist up at Sixtieth and Park. (I don't remember how we happened to choose that one. We may have discussed church architecture with Brendan Gill of the Landmarks Preservation Commission.) There were no snags there. The whole thing went through like a dose of salts, as the saying goes.

(Except that the minister and I would become good friends, and he would invite me to say a few words during a Christmas Eve service along with the comedian Joey Adams, and he and the congregation would eventually come to a parting of the ways, and one of his offenses, supposedly, was having lent the pulpit to a known atheist, who was me and not Joey Adams. He has another church now, and we correspond some about spiritual matters, and he came to the world premiere of Edgar Grana's and my requiem mass in Buffalo.)

Jill and I had our reception at the Regency Hotel, only a block north of the church. (If you have your reception at the Regency, including the cake, they throw in the bridal suite for the night; my grandchildren were stashed there during the ceremony.) That was eleven years ago now, and our understanding then was that I had had enough children (three of my own and three adopted nephews). But after a while we adopted a darling infant (three days old) named Lily, who has become my principal companion. (She will be a lazy artist when she grows up, since I celebrate every creation of hers as though it were Michelangelo's *Pietà* or the ceiling of the Sistine Chapel.)

Jill turned fifty this year and Lily is about to turn eight. I gave Jill a birthday party and also presented her with a Festschrift, a collection of sentimental essays and poems and jokes and salutations from friends and relatives. (I also told her that she was by far the oldest woman I had ever lived with.) My preface to the Festschrift began:

"To whom it may concern:

"Find here an artifact from the first year of the last decade of the second thousand years since the birth of Jesus Christ, a celebration on paper of the fiftieth birthday of my dear gifted wife Jill Krementz on February 19, 1990, a Monday. A dinner party for about fifty of her friends and relatives was held that night at Tavern on the Green in Central Park on the Island of Manhattan.

"Jill was born on that same island, but was raised, the daughter of Virginia and Walter Krementz, in Morristown, New Jersey. On the day she was born I myself was a senior at Shortridge High School in Indianapolis, who would enter Cornell University in the fall to study chemistry. Pearl Harbor would be bombed when I was nineteen and she was two months shy of being two.

"At fifty Jill looked and acted like an idealized heiress to a great American fortune who was perhaps thirty-two. She in fact went to private schools and vacationed with heirs and heiresses, but would never be one herself. Everything she owned at fifty she earned as a photographer and a creator of books for children (e.g., *A Very Young Dancer*) and books about children experiencing profound distress (e.g., *How It Feels When a Parent Dies*).

"We met in 1970 during the production of my play *Happy Birthday, Wanda June* at the Theatre de Lys in Greenwich Village. She had by then worked her way around the world, become the first female staff photographer for a New York daily paper, the *Herald Tribune,* spent a year taking photographs in South Vietnam with the war going on, and published an ethnographic and photographic masterpiece, *Sweet Pea: A Black Girl Growing Up in the Rural South,* dedicated to one of her teachers, who was Margaret Mead. But she was living in, shall we say, something less than Buckingham Palace. She was four flights up and no elevator, over a delicatessen on First Avenue just below Fifty-fourth Street.

"She told me about one would-be swain, and I guess there were a lot of those, who could not even say hello for ten minutes after climbing those stairs.

"Jill was born on the cusp between the signs of Aquarius the Water Bearer and Pisces the Fishes. She was born to be a good swimmer, if a lazy one, and to prefer water to wine. The most significant cusp in her case, though, was the one which separated virtual patriarchy in this country from the Women's Liberation Movement. It coincided with Jill's blossoming into womanhood. So she dared to behave in the workplace and during business transactions as though her gender, despite her sensational good looks, were immaterial. Whatever a man got in the way of pay and respect for doing approximately what she did, she wanted, too. She usually got it, causing not a few people to remark that she was unladylike.

"After graduating from the Masters School in Dobbs Ferry,

New York, in 1958, Jill made Manhattan and then the whole world her university. Whatever the lesson, she earned her own way, at first accepting any sort of office work which would put her among editors and journalists. She took only one formal university course, which was in anthropology at Columbia.

"Before that her particular heroine was Margaret Bourke-White, who took all the chances that male photographers were taking for *Life* magazine, and whose pictures were as good as or better than theirs. Margaret Mead was Jill's second heroine, and thus did she become, long before I met her, not only a photojournalist but a first-rate social scientist. She had to wait until she was almost fifty, and so did I, for thoughtful people of academic influence to look at all the books that she had created for or about Americans under the age of sixteen and realize that she had few peers in her understanding of the pains and satisfactions of growing up.

"We could be thankful on her fiftieth birthday, moreover, that her education had been so informal. She had no choice, praise God, but to accept what young people had to say about life at face value, since she was without training which would have empowered her to explain and interpret and footnote simply everything. All she felt entitled to do was record what the kids said, for better or for worse, and take their photographs.

"Her books aren't theory. They are evidence, take it or leave it, wholly organic, growing out of the topsoil of this moist, blue-green planet like an apple tree.

"Scientists of the future will want to know if any of the photographs of Jill in this book have been retouched. No. Let them explain, if they can, why it was that the older she was the more beautiful she became."

The Festschrift ended with this clever sonnet, "To Jill Turning Fifty," by one of Jill's favorite photographic subjects, the man of letters John Updike:

Fates Worse Than Death

The comely soul of self-effacement, you
can be admired as the twinkle in
a thousand authors' eyes where you, unseen,
perform behind the camera. How do
you soften up those hardened visages,
all pickled in the brine of daily words?—
Eudora, Tennessee, Anaïs, Kurt,
Saul, Gore, Bill, Jim, Joan, Truman, Toni, Liz?

And children, too, grow docile in your lens,
and stare like lilies toward your clicking sun
while how it feels to be a very young
whatever is elicited. Now ends
your fifth decade. Live henceforth, Leica queen,
as Jill all candlelit, the seeress seen.

X

John Updike lectured in Indianapolis soon after Jill's fiftieth birthday. Before he went, he asked me what he should know about the city of my birth. I said that I myself had become a stranger there when Jill was an itty-bitty baby. "I get invited out there to lecture, too," I said, "and when I go I don't feel as though I'm going home." It was one more nice enough American city where nice people would come to hear me. There would be some people who knew me from long ago, or whose parents did, but that could happen to Updike, too. I didn't have to go to my hometown for that to be the case, and neither did he. I had met old high school classmates or their children in San Diego, in Portland, Oregon, in Iowa City, in Manhattan.

(The sublime actress Meryl Streep, whom I had never met, came up to me in a movie theater lobby one time to tell me that she had been the roommate at Vassar of the daughter of a girl I used to date in high school.)

The Class of 1940 of Shortridge High School had its Fiftieth Reunion recently, and those in charge sent out a list of members who had vanished entirely as far as Indianapolis was concerned. I was able to report back that one of them was anything but a ghost to fellow biochemists in Boston, where he was an expert on the aging process. Another, I wrote, was a good deal more than a memory to music people in New York City, since he was a manager of the musical estates of Richard Rodgers and Oscar Hammerstein.

(I didn't go to the reunion. I was afraid of it because, like everybody else, I had had some really lousy times in high school. I probably would have gone anyway and had a swell time and lots of laughs. But then I was lucky enough to come down with the disease of the moment in the Hamptons, which was Lyme disease. I get sick only when it's useful, knock on wood. Viral pneumonia got me out of trying to be a chemist in 1942. I went briefly apeshit in the 1980s in an effort to get out of life entirely, and wound up playing Eightball in a locked ward for thirty days instead.)

I told John that Indianapolis, as far as I knew, was the only human settlement in all of history whose location was determined by a pen and a straightedge. The new State of Indiana was approximately a rectangle, but with a jagged bottom edge which had been scrawled by water obeying gravity, not by men. Men next drew on a map a great X, connecting the corners of the new state with diagonals. Where the diagonals intersected, no matter what was there, there would be the capital, whose name was to be Indianapolis. And it came to pass. (There was no navigable waterway there for cheap transportation, but the railroads would find it quick enough.)

The city-to-be was laid out on featureless land as flat as a pool table (Eightball, anybody?), according to a plan by the French-born architect Pierre Charles L'Enfant, who had designed yet another arbitrarily chosen capital, Washington, D.C. "John," I said, "it is an infinitely expandable chessboard of identical squares, each block one-tenth of a mile long, with all streets running exactly east and west or north and south, and with a circle in the middle." (Shades of the Euclidean idealism of the French Revolution, whose child I sometimes think I am.)

I used to be a halfway decent chess player (until my brains turned to tapioca). When telling John about a city he had never seen, I realized that it really was like a chessboard on which games were played out, with this piece gone and then that one (me and my big brother and my sister and our parents all leaving the board in one match). And then the pieces were set up again, but with new identities. I gave John the names of some of the more famous persons, past and present, who had been pieces on that board. "James Whitcomb Riley," I said, "Charles Manson, Richard Lugar, Steve McQueen, Dan Quayle, Kin Hubbard, Booth Tarkington, Jane Pauley, the Reverend Jim Jones of Kool-Aid fame." (I added that George Bush's making Dan Quayle the custodian of our nation's destiny, should Bush become seriously impaired, was proof to me that Bush didn't give a damn what became of the rest of us once he himself was gone. There's a bomber pilot for you.)

And my memories of Indianapolis are skewed now by the death of my war buddy Bernard V. O'Hare. He had a tenuous connection with Indianapolis. We met when we were soldiers at Camp Atterbury, which was located in the boondocks just south of there. The first time I saw him he was smoking and reading a biography of Clarence Darrow, the brilliant defense attorney. (The last time I saw him he was still smoking. The last time *anybody* saw him alive he was still smoking.) We had just become members of Headquarters Company, 2nd Battalion, 423rd Regiment, 106th Infantry Division. ("Dear Mom and Dad: Guess where I am now.") We both had some college before going into the Army. He had had Basic Training in the Infantry, bayonets and grenades and machine guns and mortars and all that. I had been trained as a virtuoso on the 240-millimeter howitzer, then the largest mobile fieldpiece. No Divisions had such humongous weapons, which were the playthings of Corps and Armies.

There were thousands upon thousands of college kids like O'Hare and me (and Norman Mailer), who were called up all at once, and who were intellectually qualified for Officer Candidate School (or to be bombardiers, for that matter). But there was no need for any more officer candidates at that time, except for those whose parents had strong political connections.

After Basic Training, nobody knew quite what to do with the likes of us. So we were sent back to college for a few months, in uniform, without hope of promotion, in the Army Specialized Training Program (ASTP). O'Hare came to the 106th from the Alabama Polytechnic Institute, and I from Carnegie Tech and then the University of Tennessee. (Assigning us to this or that college was done in haste. In one ASTP unit I heard about, everybody's last name began with H.)

We were yanked out of college again when what the Army needed, with the invasion of Europe in prospect, was riflemen and more riflemen. So there O'Hare and I were, striking up our first conversation just south of Indianapolis. The Army had instituted what it called the "Buddy System." Every Private or PFC was told to pick somebody else in his squad to know about and care about, since nobody else was going to do that. The show of concern had to be reciprocal, of course, and nobody was to be left a bachelor. (The Buddy System was a lot like the mass marriages performed in Madison Square Garden much later by the Reverend Sun Myung Moon.) So O'Hare and I got hitched, so to speak. A lot of couples were funnier-looking than us, believe you me.

The 106th Division, formerly of South Carolina, had been stripped of all its Privates and PFCs, who had been shipped overseas as replacements. But it still had all its officers and noncoms, every last one of them. All it needed was more bodies of the lowest grade. In we came by the busload, all college kids. As in the ASTP, there was no way to get promoted. (Next to the firebombing of Dresden, that might have been the most instructive thing that happened to me in World War II.)

O'Hare and I were made battalion intelligence scouts, of which there were six in each battalion. We were supposed to sneak out ahead of our lines in combat and steal peeks at the enemy without their catching us. O'Hare got the job because he had been taught how to do that during Basic. I got it, I think, because my dossier from Cornell ROTC had come right along with me, because I was wholly unfamiliar with Infantry weapons and techniques, and because I was practically invisible, being only six feet, three inches tall. I never told anybody but O'Hare about my lack of Infantry training, since somebody might have decided that I'd better have some, and it would have been unpleasant. Besides, I didn't want to leave O'Hare.

One nice thing: Camp Atterbury was so close to Indianapolis that I was able to sleep in my own bedroom and use the family car on weekends. But Mother died on one of those. My sister Alice gave birth to Mother's first grandchild (whom I would adopt along with his two brothers when he was fourteen) maybe six weekends after that, about the time of the D Day landings in France.

So our fucked-up division finally went overseas, and wound up defending seventy-five miles of front in a snowstorm against the last big German attack of the war. The Germans wore white, while we were very easy to spot, since our uniforms were the color of dogshit. We didn't have much to fight with. We were supposed to get combat boots, but they never came. The only grenades I could find were incendiaries, making O'Hare and me a couple of potential firebugs. I never saw one of our own tanks or planes. We might as well have been the Polish Cavalry fighting a blitzkrieg back in 1939. So we lost. (What else *could* we do?)

Many years later, Irwin Shaw, who had written a great novel about the war in Europe, *The Young Lions* (but who never made it into the American Academy and Institute of Arts and Letters), said to me with all possible frankness that he had never even *heard* of my division. He had sure heard of all the rest of them. But we were big news in Indianapolis, which felt that we were sort of *its* division, since we had trained so close by. We were heroes there.

(Other Indianapolis heroes: the brave crewmen of the Cruiser *Indianapolis*, which delivered to Guam the first atomic bomb, which was then dropped on Hiroshima. The *Indianapolis* was then sunk by Japanese suicide planes, and a large number of the survivors were eaten alive by sharks. How was *that* for war, when compared with the show business attacks on little countries staged by Reagan and Bush to take our minds off the crimes of their closest friends and biggest campaign contributors?)

So O'Hare and I remained a happily married couple throughout our prisoner-of-war experience. (There are pictures in the Appendix of how we looked at the very end of that. Everybody in them is a college kid who wound up as a badly beaten and wholly unarmed and leaderless former rifleman.) After the war, and although we married women, each of us continued to care about where the other one was, and how the other one was, and what he was doing and so on, and make jokes, until a little past midnight on June 9, 1990, a date which for me will live forever in infamy. That is when my buddy died.

A little more about Indianapolis, not the Cruiser but the city:

I was lucky to have been born there. (Charles Manson *wasn't* lucky to have been born there. Like so many people, he wasn't lucky to have been born anywhere.) That city gave me a free primary and secondary education richer and more humane than anything I would get from any of the five universities I attended (Cornell, Butler, Carnegie Tech, Tennessee, and Chicago). It had a widespread system of free libraries whose attendants seemed to my young mind to be angels of fun with information. There were cheap movie houses and jazz joints everywhere. There was a fine symphony orchestra, and I took lessons from Ernst Michaelis, its first-chair clarinet. (A few years ago I wound up with Benny Goodman in somebody else's car after a party. I was able to tell him truthfully, "Mr. Goodman, I used to play a little licorice-stick myself.")

In Indianapolis back then, it was only the really *dumb* rich kids who got sent away to prep school. (I knew some of them, and after they graduated from Andover or Exeter or St. Paul's or wherever, they were *still* dumb and rich.) So I was astonished and annoyed, when I took up permanent residence in the East, to meet so many people who thought it only common sense that they be allowed to set the moral and intellectual tone for this country because they had been to prep school. (It was my personal misfortune that so many of them had become literary critics. I'm about to be judged by Deerfield Academy? Deerfield *Academy?* Give me a break!)

Back to Bernard V. O'Hare again:

One of the several laudatory obituaries he received in newspapers in Northampton County, Pennsylvania, said (far down in the story), "Along with author Kurt Vonnegut, with whom he trained, he was imprisoned in Dresden when it was firebombed." (One obituary called him "one of the most admired and colorful attorneys in Northampton County," and another called him "feisty.") About a month before he died, I spoke about the firebombing at the National Air and Space Museum in Washington, D.C. Mine was one of a series of lectures entitled "The Legacy of Strategic Bombing," and it began as follows:

"It isn't usual for a speech to begin with a disclaimer. The first rule of public speaking is 'Never apologize.'

"In my case, though, since I have been asked to speak about the firebombing of a German city, and my name is obviously German in origin, it seems prudent to say that I was and remain unsympathetic to the enthusiasms of the Nazi war machine, as was my commanding general, another German-American, Dwight David Eisenhower. His German ancestors and mine became Americans decades before the Statue of Liberty was erected in New York Harbor.

"I was a battalion scout, a PFC, who was captured on the border of Germany in December 1944 during the Battle of the Bulge. Thus did I happen to be a laborer under guard in Dresden when it was firebombed on February 13, 1945. The Germans were in full retreat on all fronts and surrendering in ever greater numbers, and had few airplanes left, and every German city *but* Dresden had been bombed and bombed. The war would end soon, on May 7.

"When I was liberated in May, I was in the Russian zone. I spent some time with concentration camp survivors and heard their stories before returning to the American lines. I have since visited Auschwitz and Birkenau and have seen the collections there of human hair and children's shoes and toys and so on. I know about the Holocaust. Elie Wiesel and I are friends.

"The principal reason for this disclaimer is an assertion by that A-plus student, the heavy thinker George Will, that I trivialized the Holocaust with my novel *Slaughterhouse-Five*. I find that most unhelpful, and I hope you do, too.

"There is no dearth of persons who could tell you what it is like to be unarmed in a mainly civilian population bombed or rocketed or whatever from the air. There are surely millions of us by now. The most recent initiates into our enormous club are in some of the poorer neighborhoods of Panama City. Cambodians and Vietnamese are senior members now.

"How many people in this very room here, in fact, have, while not in combat, been attacked from the air? (About twelve.)

"The firebombing of Dresden was mainly a British enterprise. Americans, several of whom I have since met, dropped high explosives in the daytime to make kindling for the thousands of incendiaries to come. The British came that night with the incendiaries. Their target? The whole city. It was hard to miss. And the city became one flame, with tornadoes dancing in the suburbs like whirling dervishes. The man who interviewed me for admission to the University of Chicago after the war was one of the Americans who attacked in the daytime, virtually unopposed. He said, 'We hated to do it.'

"Most of the British, I think, felt otherwise. They wanted revenge for the London blitz and the leveling of Coventry and the humiliation at Dunkirk and so on. The Americans had no scores to settle. They might have felt vengeful if they had known the incredible extent of the horrors of the German death camps, but that hadn't been discovered yet by the outside world.

"What Americans had to avenge was Pearl Harbor. They would do that, with no help from the British, in their own sweet time. Like the British, they would do it when the war was already clearly won.

"The total destruction of Hiroshima, a racist atrocity of atrocities, nonetheless had military significance. When I was in Tokyo with William Styron a few years ago, he said, 'Thank God for the atomic bomb. If it weren't for it, I would be dead.' When the bomb dropped, he was a Marine in Okinawa, preparing for the invasion of the Japanese home islands. It seems certain to me that many more Americans and Japanese would have died during the invasion than were burned to crisps at Hiroshima.

"The firebombing of Dresden was an emotional event without a trace of military importance. The Germans purposely kept the city free of major war industries and arsenals and troop concentrations so that it might be a safe haven for the wounded and refugees. There were no air-raid shelters to speak of and few antiaircraft guns. It was a famous world art treasure, like Paris or Vienna or Prague, and about as sinister as a wedding cake. I will say again what I have often said in print and in speeches, that not one Allied soldier was able to advance as much as an inch because of the firebombing of Dresden. Not one prisoner of the Nazis got out of prison a microsecond earlier. Only one person on earth clearly benefited, and I am that person. I got about five dollars for each corpse, counting my fee tonight.

"Nobody ever argues with me very plausibly or very long when I say that, and I've said it not only here but in Britain and France and Scandinavia and Poland and Czechoslovakia and Germany. I may have said it in Mexico. I can't remember whether or not I've ever said it in Mexico.

"Paradoxically, I am not only the one success of the raid but also one of its thousands of failures. Everything possible was done to make me die, but I did not die. It wasn't as though the bombardiers knew where I was and were careful not to hurt me. They didn't know or care who was what or where. The leaders of their nations hoped they would burn down the city and kill as many people of any sort as they could with fire or smoke or lack of oxygen, or some combination of the three.

"Same scheme as Hiroshima, but with primitive technology, and with white people down below.

"I fully understand the bombardiers' lack of discrimination as to who or what was underneath them. They had a point: Whoever was down there, whether by actively supporting Hitler or simply failing to overthrow him, was directly or indirectly playing a part, however small, in Nazi crimes against humanity. I, and the ninety-nine other American privates in my particular labor detail there in Dresden, were working in a factory that made a malt syrup laced with vitamins which was for pregnant women, who would give birth to more heartless warriors. At least we weren't volunteers. We were forced to work for our keep under guard, as specified by the Articles of the Geneva Convention Respecting Prisoners of War. If we had been non-coms or officers, we wouldn't have had to work and would have been not in Dresden but in some big prison out in the country-side.

"I have said that I have so far received about five bucks for every corpse created by the firestorm. But this is a ballpark figure if there ever was one. It will never be known how many corpses there were or what sorts of souls may have inhabited them. I have heard every number from 35,000 to 200,000. The highest and lowest estimates are politically motivated, minimizing or maximizing the viciousness of the raid. The number which sounds right to me, and the one most often heard from people with no axes to grind, is 135,000, more than were killed in Hiroshima. But the population of Dresden at the time of the raid was a mystery, since so many refugees from the collapsing

Russian Front and other bombed cities were arriving day after day.

"After the raid, the corpses, most of them in ordinary cellars, were so numerous and represented such a health hazard that they were cremated on huge funeral pyres, or by flamethrowers whose nozzles were thrust into the cellars, without being counted or identified. Many friends and relatives of refugees newly arrived in Dresden can say of them nowadays only that they somehow disappeared near the end of World War II. The town was full of Polish slave laborers. Their friends and relatives must be saying of them nowadays simply that they were taken off to Germany somewhere and never came home again.

"This much can be said about Dresden's population with some certainty: There were few remotely able-bodied males between the ages of sixteen and fifty. Such specimens were all fighting or surrendering or dying or deserting somewhere else. The great German writer Günter Grass, who was a boy during World War II, asked me one time in what year I was born. I told him 1922. He said that there were no males my age still alive in Germany, Austria, or the Soviet Union. That was only a slight exaggeration.

"Among the unidentified, not-even-counted dead in the cellars of Dresden there were, without doubt, war criminals or loathsomely proud relatives of war criminals, SS and Gestapo, and so on. Whatever they got was too good for them. Maybe most of the Germans killed in Dresden, excepting the infants and children, of course, got what was coming to them. I asked another great German writer, Heinrich Böll, what he thought the dangerous flaw in the character of so many Germans was, and he said, 'Obedience.'

"But I have to say that I felt no pride or satisfaction while carrying corpses from cellars to great funeral pyres while friends and relatives of the missing watched. They may have thought that it served me right to do such gruesome work at gunpoint, since it was my side in the war which had made it a necessity.

But who knows what they thought? Their minds may have been blank. I know mine was.

"And it was all such one hell of a long time ago. Forty-five years.

"The firebombing of Dresden, which had no military significance, was a work of art. It was a tower of smoke and flame to commemorate the rage and heartbreak of so many who had had their lives warped or ruined by the indescribable greed and vanity and cruelty of Germany. The British and Americans who built the tower had been raised, like me, and in response to World War I, to be pacifists.

"Two more such towers would be built by Americans alone in Japan. When they were built and then blew away, leaving nothing but ashes and cinders, I was on furlough in Indianapolis, my home. And even though I had seen on the ground the effects of a similar total conflagration, I myself regarded those twin towers as works of art. Beautiful!

"That was how crazy I had become. That is how crazy we had all become.

"That is how crazy we remain today. Attacking a civilian population from the air, with or without warning, with or without a declaration of war, has become for most of us simply one more symbol, like the Liberty Bell, of national pride.

"Who would be so chicken-hearted as to say that the killing from the air of Muammar Qaddafi's adopted daughter, as well intentioned as my own adopted daughter, was a serious matter, or even interesting? Not *The New York Times*. Not *The Washington Post*. Not MacNeil or Lehrer or Brokaw or Rather or Jennings. And not me.

"We also zapped the French Embassy.

"Henry Kissinger, winner of the Nobel Peace Prize, who recommended that Hanoi be carpet-bombed at Christmastime, is considered a grave, humane, wise diplomat. I think so, too.

"Albert Schweitzer, a physician as well as a musician and a philosopher, hoped to teach us reverence for life. He felt that we should not kill even the tiniest, most contemptible organism if we could possibly avoid doing that. On the face of it, this ideal is preposterous, since so many diseases are caused by germs. Dr. Schweitzer himself must have killed germs by the billions. Either that, or most of his patients died.

"If I were to speak tonight of the agony experienced by individual germs in the bodies of patients dosed by Dr. Schweitzer, the men in white coats would be entitled to cart me off to St. Elizabeths. And our frame of mind now, not just in this country but in many, many others, including, no doubt, Libya, is such that civilians attacked from the air are as unworthy of being discussed as individual germs.

"Many people find my speeches, and probably my books, too, hopelessly ambiguous. But I don't want to leave you feeling unfed. So let me throw these big chunks of beefsteak into your stew, so to speak, and speaking as a cold-blooded Commander in Chief:

"Should Dresden have been firebombed? No.

"Should Hamburg have been bombed and bombed? Yes.

"Should Hiroshima have been bombed? Ask all those who would have been dead otherwise.

"Should Nagasaki have been bombed? No.

"Should Hanoi's civilian population have been bombed and bombed? No.

"Should any part of Cambodia have been bombed? No.

"Should Libya have been attacked from the air? No. That was show biz.

"Should Panama City have been bombed? No. That was more show biz.

"I thank you for your attention."

There was no press coverage of my wonderful remarks, although their auspices were reputable. (I don't whimper about this. I notice.) I was well-known. The National Air and Space Museum was well-known. The firebombing of Dresden was well-known. In combination, you would think, some reporter might have found us interesting. Another American ex-PW who was in Dresden with me and O'Hare showed up unexpectedly, and testified from the audience that all I said was true. And my adopted seven-year-old daughter Lily was sitting near him with my wife Jill. I had Lily stand up on her seat as an approximation of the sort of germ Muammar Qaddafi's adopted daughter had been before we killed her with the very latest in air-to-ground weapons technology. Some people might argue that my equation was misleading, since Qaddafi's kid was an infant and mine would soon be eight years old.

We got no press coverage, in my opinion (although there was an overflow audience in the lobby watching on TV screens) because in Washington, D.C., citizens who say that our air power has been or ever could be misused are regarded by those who decide what is news and what isn't as politically immature, like a lot of college kids and unlike Dr. Henry Kissinger, Nobel Laureate for Peace. When all is said and done, we are simple-minded creatures, glad to believe on the basis of symbolism alone (up is better than down) that air superiority is moral superiority. (After all, look where God lives. He isn't in some ditch like the Vietnam Veterans Memorial.) What can I accomplish but a decrease in American happiness if I say to a crowd, as I did, that an attack on a civilian population by clean, decent young men in enormously expensive and complex flying machines is, when viewed from the ground, no different from the practice of the world's worst police departments, which is to make arrested nobodies watch the torture of innocent friends and relatives, young and old, with the intention of changing the nobodies' probable politics?

A woman said to me after my speech, "Nobody should *ever* be bombed."

I replied, "Nothing could be more obvious."

XI

The fellow ex–Dresden PW at my National Air and Space Museum lecture was Tom Jones, who had paired off (as ordered) in his 106th Division platoon with Joe Crone, the model for Billy Pilgrim, the leading character in *Slaughterhouse-Five.* Jones said, in a letter I got only yesterday, "I remember Crone in Camp Atterbury. When we went on a forced march I had to walk behind him and pick up all the utensils falling out of his backpack. He could never do it right.

"I bunked with him when he died. One morning he woke up and his head was swollen like a watermelon and I talked him into going on sick call. By midday word came back that he had died. You remember we slept two in a bunk so I had to shake Crone several times a night and say, 'Let's turn over.' I recall how in the early morning hours the slop cans at the end of the barracks overflowed. Everyone had the shits, and it flowed down the barracks under everyone's bunk. The Germans never would give us more cans."

Joe Crone is buried somewhere in Dresden wearing a white

paper suit. He let himself starve to death before the firestorm. In *Slaughterhouse-Five* I have him return home to become a fabulously well-to-do optometrist. (Jones and Crone were stockpiled college kids like O'Hare and me. We all read a lot at Camp Atterbury.)

Jones, there in Washington, D.C., turned out to have been quite a packrat when it came to wartime memorabilia. He had a copy of a letter given to us by the Germans which urged us to join their army (and get plenty to eat) and go fight for civilization on the Russian Front. (Rumor was that five Americans somewhere else had accepted the offer. If those five didn't exist we would still have had to invent them.) Tom Jones had photographs of several of us, including O'Hare (but not Joe Crone, not Billy Pilgrim), taken right after the war ended. Our guards had disappeared, and the Russian Army had not yet arrived, and we found ourselves in the valley I describe at the end of my novel *Bluebeard* (called *Bluebird* in the meticulously edited *New York Times*). We came upon a German Army wagon with horse still attached and made it ours. We painted white American stars on its sides and "USA" on its tailgate, so the Russian fighter planes overhead wouldn't shoot at us. We traveled that way for several days until the Russian ground troops finally arrived and locked us up again.

Another thing I have put into the Appendix was handed me by a stranger in the audience. It is from a "Bomber's Baedeker" from World War II. It tells you where (the choice is yours) you might want to drop bombs if for one reason or another you have some or all of them left over from that day's or night's mission. (Waste not, want not.) The donor of the document (obviously another chicken-hearted person) wanted me to confirm what I could only assert up to then: that Dresden was no more a military target than Kalamazoo, Michigan, is today. There is a lot of stuff in Kalamazoo. There was a lot of stuff in Dresden, businesses and forms of transportation and police stations and facilities for generating electricity and giving birth to potential soldiers and nurses and so on. (Bombs away!) There was a zoo in Dresden for the entertainment of potential soldiers and nurses. The Baedeker for Bombers missed that one, but the bombs didn't. You should have seen the giraffe after the firestorm. (I did.)

During the question-and-answer period following my great speech I found an opportunity to quote O'Hare. When a Liberty Ship (the *Lucretia C. Mott,* named for a women's rights advocate) had wallowed us back to the United States through severe storms in the North Atlantic, and it was time for me and my buddy to say good-bye for a while (a condition now quite permanent), I said to him, "What did you learn?" The future DA O'Hare replied, "I will never again believe my Government." This had to do with our Government's tall tales of delicate surgery performed by bombers equipped with Sperry and Norden bombsights. These instruments were so precise, we had been told, that a bombardier could drop his billets-doux down the chimney of a factory if ordered to. There were solemn charades performed for newsreels in which military policemen with drawn .45 automatics escorted bombardiers carrying bombsights to their planes. That was how desperate the Germans and the Japanese were (so went the message) to learn and make use of the secret of our bombings' diabolical accuracy themselves.

Such a sop to civilian sensibilities nowadays would seem as unintentionally hilarious as a love scene between Gloria Swanson and Rudolph Valentino. Consider the flying machines built since World War II on exhibit at the National Air and Space Museum. Everybody knows that the main business of the manufacturers of all of them has been the creation of devices both manned and unmanned whose purpose is to kill everything, whether animal or vegetable, within an enormous radius. (I am aware that the Soviet Union has made the same sorts of doomsday darts.)

I was told sotto voce by a female museologist (with great legs) at Air and Space that the museum's biggest supporters (weapons manufacturers) were not happy to have strategic bombing (dead and wounded civilians) discussed on that particular property, even though Tom Jones's and my gloom was about to be dispelled by the sunshine of General Curtis LeMay, retired commander of the Strategic Air Command (who wanted to bomb North Vietnam back to the Stone Age). Why bring up the subject at all? They felt that the emphasis should be on high-speed transportation ("on errands not conspicuously improved," according to Henry David Thoreau) and the exploration of space. Before my speech, in fact, my daughter Lily (later to be a stand-in for Muammar Qaddafi's much younger dead Arab kid) watched a little bit of a movie about the opportunities in space, narrated by Walter Cronkite. (I know him. I know everybody.) Yes, and I may now have put my finger (although I doubt it) on why President George Bush took no notice in public of the departure of *Voyager 2* from its native Solar System forever ("My work is done"). A whole lot of proud and well-heeled (thanks to the public treasury) voters in the space boondoggle might be thrown out of work (homeless) if it became generally known that the dove (*Voyager 2*) we sent out from this Ark floating in a flood of nothingness reported that there was only death and more death out there.

Also: Children and neighbors of planet wreckers (polluters and clear-cutters and destroyers of salt marshes, and uranium miners and so on) might start looking at them askance if the President drew attention to the fact that this is the only inhabitable planet available to us within the next trillion years, give or take a few. (I am aware that everybody laughed at Christopher Columbus, who opened a lightly defended hemisphere to piracy and privateering which go on to this very day. Ever talk to a Hopi selling jewelry in a hotel lobby out in Santa Fe?) If I haven't said so in print before (and I can't stand to read myself), let me say now that most people find life so hard and disappointing (because they can't make money or they hate their jobs or they can't dance or can't have as much fun fucking as we're all supposed to, or they are no good at sports or are just plain sick, or their kids are a mess, or their mates hate them the way Xanthippe hated Socrates and Father's mate hated him) that they don't care if life goes on or not. So that is one reason why repairing this sinking Ark (with half the animals dead already) will be urgently discussed in some quarters but never implemented. (Christopher Lehmann-Haupt, a *New York Times* daily book reviewer, told me at a party maybe five years ago that he couldn't stand to read me anymore, so that makes two of us.)

So when the American ad agency for Volkswagen asked me (along with several other fogbound futurologists) to compose a letter to Earthlings a century from now which would be used in a series of institutional ads in *Time* (no friends of mine), I wrote as follows:

"Ladies & Gentlemen of A.D. 2088:

"It has been suggested that you might welcome words of wisdom from the past, and that several of us in the twentieth century should send you some. Do you know this advice from Polonius in Shakespeare's *Hamlet*: 'This above all: to thine own self be true'? Or what about these instructions from St. John the Divine: 'Fear God, and give glory to Him; for the hour of His judgment has come'? The best advice from my own era for you or for just about anybody anytime, I guess, is a prayer first used by alcoholics who hoped to never take a drink again: 'God grant me the serenity to accept the things I cannot change, courage to change the things I can, and wisdom to know the difference.'

"Our century hasn't been as free with words of wisdom as some others, I think, because we were the first to get reliable information about the human situation: how many of us there were, how much food we could raise or gather, how fast we were reproducing, what made us sick, what made us die, how much damage we were doing to the air and water and topsoil on which most life forms depended, how violent and heartless nature can be, and on and on. Who could wax wise with so much bad news pouring in?

"For me, the most paralyzing news was that Nature was no conservationist. It needed no help from us in taking the planet apart and putting it back together some different way, not necessarily improving it from the viewpoint of living things. It set fire to forests with lightning bolts. It paved vast tracts of arable land with lava, which could no more support life than big-city parking lots. It had in the past sent glaciers down from the North Pole to grind up major portions of Asia, Europe, and North America. Nor was there any reason to think that it wouldn't do that again someday. At this very moment it is turning African farms to deserts, and can be expected to heave up tidal waves or shower down white-hot boulders from outer space at any time. It has not only exterminated exquisitely evolved species in a twinkling, but drained oceans and drowned continents as well. If people think Nature is their friend, then they sure don't need an enemy.

"Yes, and as you people a hundred years from now must know full well, and as your grandchildren will know even better: Nature is ruthless when it comes to matching the quantity of life in any given place at any given time to the quantity of nourishment available. So what have you and Nature done about overpopulation? Back here in 1988, we were seeing ourselves as a new sort of glacier, warm-blooded and clever, unstoppable, about to gobble up everything and then make love—and then double in size again.

"On second thought, I am not sure I could bear to hear what you and Nature may have done about too many people for too small a food supply.

"And here is a crazy idea I would like to try on you: Is it possible that we aimed rockets with hydrogen bomb warheads at each other, all set to go, in order to take our minds off the deeper problem—how cruelly Nature can be expected to treat us, Nature being Nature, in the by-and-by?

"Now that we can discuss the mess we are in with some precision, I hope you have stopped choosing abysmally ignorant optimists for positions of leadership. They were useful only so long as nobody had a clue as to what was really going on— during the past seven million years or so. In my time, they have been catastrophic as heads of sophisticated institutions with real work to do.

"The sort of leaders we need now are not those who promise ultimate victory over Nature through perseverance in living as we do right now, but those with the courage and intelligence to present to the world what appear to be Nature's stern but reasonable surrender terms:

1. Reduce and stabilize your population.
2. Stop poisoning the air, the water, and the topsoil.
3. Stop preparing for war and start dealing with your real problems.
4. Teach your kids, and yourselves, too, while you're at it, how to inhabit a small planet without helping to kill it.
5. Stop thinking science can fix anything if you give it a trillion dollars.
6. Stop thinking your grandchildren will be OK no matter how wasteful or destructive you may be, since they can go to a nice new planet on a spaceship. That is *really* mean and stupid.
7. And so on. Or else.

"Am I too pessimistic about life a hundred years from now? Maybe I have spent too much time with scientists and not enough time with speechwriters for politicians. For all I know, even bag ladies and bag gentlemen will have their own personal helicopters or rocket belts in A.D. 2088. Nobody will have to leave home to go to work or school, or even stop watching television. Everybody will sit around all day punching the keys of computer terminals connected to everything there is, and sip orange drink through straws like the astronauts."

So ends my letter to the people of 2088. Lily Vonnegut might still be alive to receive it. But she would be 105 years old by then! As though I hadn't already given the world more than enough reasons to feel miserable, I sold this bouquet of sunbeams and bubbling laughter to *Lear's* magazine:

"In the children's fable *The White Deer,* by the late American humorist James Thurber, the Royal Astronomer in a medieval court reports that all the stars are going out. What has really happened is that the astronomer has grown old and is going blind. That was Thurber's condition, too, when he wrote his tale. He was making fun of a sort of old poop who imagined that life was ending not merely for himself but for the whole universe. Inspired by Thurber, then, I choose to call any old poop who writes a popular book saying that the world, or at least his own country, is done for, a 'Royal Astronomer' and his subject matter 'Royal Astronomy.'

"Since I myself have become an old poop at last, perhaps I, too, should write such a book. But it is hard for me to follow the standard formula for successful Royal Astronomy, a formula going back who knows how far, maybe to the invention of printing by the Chinese a couple of thousand years ago. The formula is, of course: 'Things aren't as good as they used to be. The young people don't know anything and don't want to know anything. We have entered a steep decline!'

"But have we? Back when I was a kid, lynchings of black people were reported almost every week, and always went unpunished. Apartheid was as sternly enforced in my hometown, which was Indianapolis, as it is in South Africa nowadays. Many great universities, including those in the Ivy League, rejected most of the Jews who applied for admission solely because of their Jewishness, and had virtually no Jews and absolutely no blacks, God knows, on their faculties.

"I am going to ask a question—and President Reagan, please don't answer: Those were the *good old days*?

"When I was a kid during the Great Depression, when it was being demonstrated most painfully that prosperity was not a natural by-product of liberty, books by Royal Astronomers were as popular as they are today. They said, as most of them do today, that the country was falling apart because the young people were no longer required to read Plato and Aristotle and Marcus Aurelius and St. Augustine and Montaigne and the like, whose collective wisdom was the foundation of any decent and just and productive society.

"Back in the Great Depression, the Royal Astronomers used to say that a United States deprived of that wisdom was nothing but a United States of radio quiz shows and music straight out of the jungles of Darkest Africa. They say now that the same subtraction leaves us a United States of nothing but television quiz shows and rock and roll, which leads, they say, inexorably to dementia. But I find uncritical respect for most works by great thinkers of long ago unpleasant, because they almost all accepted as natural and ordinary the belief that females and minority races and the poor were on earth to be uncomplaining, hardworking, respectful, and loyal servants of white males, who did the important thinking and exercised leadership.

"Such wisdom is a foundation on which only white males can build. And there is a lot of it in the Holy Bible, I'm sorry to say.

"I went to a big luncheon last week for a vice-president of the filmmakers' union of the USSR, a kind and hopeful man as nearly as I could tell. Everybody was asking him about *glasnost* and all that. Would there really be more freedom in his country? And what about all the political prisoners still in the gulag and the mental hospitals? And what about the Jews who weren't allowed to emigrate? And so on.

"The experiment with more freedom and justice was just beginning, he said, but there were encouraging signs in the arts. All sorts of suppressed books and movies were being released. The demand was so great for writings previously taboo, he said, that there was a terrific paper shortage. Artists and intellectuals were elated. But most ordinary workers, to whom freedom of expression wasn't so important, were waiting to see if *glasnost* was somehow going to get them better food and shelter and clothing, and cars and appliances and other things of that sort, which, unfortunately, were not among the inevitable results of increased freedom.

"Alcoholism continues to make a lot of trouble over there, just as alcoholism and cocaine addiction are making a lot of trouble over here. Both are severe public-health problems not notably responsive to whether the sufferer is politically free or not.

"So what is going on over there is really a touching thing for us to watch and hear about, an honest effort to give the common people of a powerful nation more liberty than they or their ancestors have ever known. If the experiment goes on for any length of time—and just a few people could shut it down instantly—we can expect to see it dawn on the citizens of the Soviets that liberty, like virtue, is its own reward, which can be a disappointment. There as here and, in fact, almost everywhere on the planet, the great mass of human beings yearns for rewards that are more substantial.

"After that lunch I pondered my own country's continuing experiments with liberty, which have been going on for more than two centuries. The Soviet Union has been a Workers' Paradise only since 1922, coincidentally the same year I was born into this so-called Beacon of Liberty to the Rest of the World.

"And I said to the guest of honor, through an interpreter, that maybe the Soviet Union wasn't doing half badly, since in my own country slavery was perfectly legal for almost a hundred years after the signing of the Declaration of Independence. I said that even the saintly Thomas Jefferson owned slaves.

"I did not mention our genocide of Indians back in my great-grandfather's time. That would have been too much. I talk about that and think about that as little as possible. Thank God it isn't taught in school much.

"Our own country has a *glasnost* experiment going on, too, of course. It consists of making women and racial minorities the equals of white males, in terms of both the civility and respect to be accorded them and their rights under the law. This would seem an abomination to the ancient wise men whose works our young people are dangerously, supposedly, neglecting in favor of rock and roll.

"A proper reply by the American people to Royal Astronomers who denounce that neglect, it seems to me, would go something like this: 'Almost none of the ancient wise men believed in real equality, and neither do you—but we believe in it.'

"Is there nothing about the United States of my youth, aside from youth itself, that I miss sorely now? There is one thing I miss so much that I can hardly stand it, which is freedom from the certain knowledge that human beings will very soon have made this moist, blue-green planet uninhabitable by human beings. There is no stopping us. We will continue to breed like rabbits. We will continue to engage in technological nincompoopery with hideous side effects unforeseen. We will make only token repairs on our cities now collapsing. We will not clean up much of the poisonous mess that we ourselves have made.

"If flying-saucer creatures or angels or whatever were to come here in a hundred years, say, and find us gone like the dinosaurs, what might be a good message for humanity to leave for them, maybe carved in great big letters on a Grand Canyon wall?

"Here is this old poop's suggestion:

WE PROBABLY COULD HAVE SAVED OURSELVES,
BUT WERE TOO DAMNED LAZY TO TRY VERY HARD.

"We might well add this:

AND TOO DAMN CHEAP.

"So it's curtains not just for me as I grow old. It's curtains for everyone. How's that for full-strength Royal Astronomy?"

XII

"MIT has played an important part in the history of my branch of the Vonnegut family. My father and grandfather took degrees in architecture here. My Uncle Pete flunked out of here. My only brother Bernard, nine years my senior, took a doctor's degree in chemistry here. Father and Grandfather became self-employed architects and partners. Uncle Pete became a building contractor, also self-employed. My brother knew early on that he would be a research scientist, and so could not be self-employed. If he was to have room enough and equipment enough to do what he did best, then he was going to have to work for somebody else. Who would that be?"

Such was what I considered a tantalizing beginning of a speech I gave at MIT back in 1985. (There have been times when I was nutty enough to believe that I might change the course of history a tiny bit, and this was one of them.) There in Kresge Auditorium I had a full house of young people who could do what the magician Merlin could only pretend to do in the Court of King Arthur, in Camelot. They could turn loose or rein in enormous forces (invisible as often as not) in the service or disservice of this or that enterprise (such as Star Wars).

"Most of you," I went on, "will soon face my brother's dilemma when he graduated from here. In order to survive and even prosper, most of you will have to make somebody else's technological dreams come true—along with your own, of course. You will have to form that mixture of dreams we call a partnership—or more romantically, a marriage.

"My brother got his doctorate in 1938, I think. If he had gone to work in Germany after that, he would have been helping to make Hitler's dreams come true. If he had gone to work in Italy, he would have been helping to make Mussolini's dreams come true. If he had gone to work in Japan, he would have been helping to make Tojo's dreams come true. If he had gone to work in the Soviet Union, he would have been helping to make Stalin's dreams come true. He went to work for a bottle manufacturer in Butler, Pennsylvania, instead. It can make quite a difference not just to you but to humanity: the sort of boss you choose, whose dreams you help come true.

"Hitler dreamed of killing Jews, Gypsies, Slavs, homosexuals, Communists, Jehovah's Witnesses, mental defectives, believers in democracy, and so on, in industrial quantities. It would have remained only a dream if it hadn't been for chemists as well educated as my brother, who supplied Hitler's executioners with the cyanide gas known as Cyklon-B. It would have remained only a dream if architects and engineers as capable as my father and grandfather hadn't designed extermination camps—the fences, the towers, the barracks, the railroad sidings, and the gas chambers and crematoria—for maximum ease of operation and efficiency. I recently visited two of those camps in Poland, Auschwitz and Birkenau. They are technologically perfect. There is only one grade I could give their designers, and that grade is A-plus. They surely solved all the problems set for them.

"Yes, and that is the grade I would have to give to the technicians who have had a hand in the creation of the car bombs which are now exploding regularly in front of embassies and department stores and movie theaters and houses of worship of every kind. They surely solve the problems set for them. *Kablooey!* A-plus! A-plus!

"Which brings us to the differences between men and women. Feminists have won a few modest successes in the United States during the past two decades, so it has become almost obligatory to say that the differences between the two sexes have been exaggerated. But this much is clear to me: Generally speaking, women don't like immoral technology nearly as much as men do. This could be the result of some hormone deficiency. Whatever the reason, women, often taking their children with them, tend to outnumber men in demonstrations against schemes and devices which can kill people. In fact, the most effective doubter of the benefits of unbridled technological advancement so far was a woman, Mary Wollstonecraft Shelley, who died 134 years ago. She, of course, created the idea of the Monster of Frankenstein.

"And to show you how fruity, how feminine I have become in late middle age: If I were the President of MIT, I would hang pictures of Boris Karloff as the Monster of Frankenstein all over the institution. Why? To remind students and faculty that humanity now cowers in muted dread, expecting to be killed sooner or later by Monsters of Frankenstein. Such killing goes on right now, by the way, in many other parts of the world, often with our sponsorship—hour after hour, day after day.

"What should be done? You here at MIT should set an example for your colleagues everywhere by writing and then taking an oath based on the Hippocratic Oath, by which medical doctors have been bound for twenty-four centuries. Do I mean to say that no physician in all that time has violated that oath? Certainly not. But every doctor who has violated it has been correctly branded a scumbag. And why has the late Josef Mengele become the most monstrous of all the Nazis, in the opinion of most of us? He was a doctor, and he gleefully violated the Hippocratic Oath.

"If some of you elect to act on my suggestion, to write a new oath, you will of course have to examine the original, which is conventionally dated 460 years before the birth of Jesus Christ. So it is a musty old Greek document, much of it irrelevant to a physician's moral dilemmas in the present day. It is also a perfectly human document. No one has ever suggested that it came from a god in a vision or on clay tablets found on a mountaintop. A person or some people wrote it, inspired by nothing more than their own wishes to help rather than harm humankind. I assume that most of you, too, would rather help than harm humankind, and might welcome formal restraints on what a wicked boss might expect of you.

"The part of the Hippocratic Oath which needs the least editing, it seems to me, is this: 'The regimen I adopt shall be for the benefit of my patients, according to my ability and judgment, and not for their hurt or for any wrong. I will give no deadly drug to any, though it be asked of me, nor will I counsel such.' You could easily paraphrase this so as to include not just doctors but every sort of scientist, remembering that all sciences have their roots in the simple wish to make people safe and well.

"Your paraphrase might go like this: 'The regimen I adopt shall be for the benefit of all life on this planet, according to my own ability and judgment, and not for its hurt or for any wrong. I will create no deadly substance or device, though it be asked of me, nor will I counsel such.'

"That might make a good beginning for an oath everyone would gladly take upon graduation from MIT. And there is surely more than that you would gladly swear to. You could take it from there.

"I thank you for your attention."

What a flop! The applause was polite enough. (There were

many Oriental faces out there. Who knows what *they* may have been thinking?) But nobody came up front afterward and said he or she was going to take a shot at writing an oath all technical people would be glad to take. There was nothing in the student paper the next week. It was all over. (If such a speech had been given at Cornell when I was a student there, I would have written an oath that very night whilst talking to myself. Then again, I had had lots of free time, since I was flunking practically everything.)

What makes the students of today so unresponsive? (Only this morning I, an old poop, got a letter asking me if I had any suggestions for a revision of the Pledge of Allegiance, and I answered by return mail: "I pledge allegiance to the Constitution of the United States of America, and the flag which is its symbol, with liberty and justice for all.") I'll tell you what makes the students so unresponsive. They know what I will never get through my head: that life is *unserious*. (Why not make Caligula's horse a Consul?)

Before my great speech to the MIT students I talked to some of them about Star Wars, Ronald Reagan's belief that laser beams and satellites and flypaper and who-knows-what could be linked together in such a way as to form an invisible dome no enemy missile could penetrate. They didn't think there was any way it could be made to operate, but they all wanted to work on it anyway. (Why *not* make Caligula's horse a Consul?)

XIII

When I studied anthropology long ago at the University of Chicago, my most famous professor was Dr. Robert Redfield. The idea that all societies evolved through similar, predictable stages on their way to higher (Victorian) civilization, from polytheism to monotheism, for instance, or from the tom-tom to the symphony orchestra, had by then been ridiculed into obscurity. It was generally agreed that there was no such ladder as cultural evolution. But Dr. Redfield said in effect, "Wait just a minute." He said that he could describe to every fair-minded person's satisfaction one (and only one) stage every society had passed through or would pass through. He called this inevitable stage and his essay on it "The Folk Society."

First of all, a Folk Society was isolated, and in an area it considered organically its own. It grew from that soil and no other. The break between the living and the dead was indistinct, and bonds of kinship crisscrossed every which way. There was such general agreement as to what life was all about and how people should behave in every conceivable situation that very little was debatable.

Dr. Redfield gave a public lecture on the Folk Society in the springtime each year. It was popular, I think, because so many of us took it as scientific advice about how to find deep and enduring contentment: join or create a Folk Society. (This was back in the 1940s, remember, long before the communes and flower children and shared music and ideals of my children's generation.) Dr. Redfield denounced sentimentality about life in Folk Societies, saying they were hell for anyone with a lively imagination or an insatiable curiosity or a need to experiment and invent—or with an irrepressible sense of the ridiculous. But I still find myself daydreaming of an isolated little gang of like-minded people in a temperate climate, in a clearing in a woodland near a lake (an ideal spot, by the way, for a daydreaming maiden to find herself the captrix of a unicorn). My son Mark would help found and bankroll such a commune in British Columbia, and later write about it in *The Eden Express*. (I said in my own *Palm Sunday* that sons try to make their mothers' impractical dreams for themselves come true. Here was a case of a son's making his father's impractical dream come true. It worked OK for a while.)

Realtors commonly imply that to buy or rent a house in such and such a locality will make the sucker eligible for virtually instant membership in a Folk Society. I had something like that in the back of my mind when I quit General Electric and moved to Cape Cod, where I lived for twenty years (Provincetown, then Osterville, then Barnstable). But I had no relatives there, and I wasn't even an Anglo-Saxon or a descendant of seafarers or colonials. And very few of my ideas, frequently subject to public inspection in magazines and books, coincided with those of my neighbors. So I was as much an outsider when I left as I had been on the day I arrived. (Soon after I arrived I offered my services as a volunteer fireman, since I had been a fireman in

Alplaus, New York, outside Schenectady. I might as well have been a freshman at Yale expressing a willingness to join Skull and Bones.)

Nor do I have any illusions that I am in any serious way a part of the picture-perfect village in which I am writing now, which is Sagaponack, Long Island. The Fire Department asks for money in a form letter to my PO box, and I send them some. My nearest neighbor is the painter Robert Dash, who boasts that his hedges are so thick he can't see anything outside his own property. (Noises can still get through his hedges, though. One time Truman Capote spent the afternoon in my backyard, talking about himself, and Dash told me later that he thought I had been visited by a garrulous maiden aunt.)

(I expected this to be an easy chapter, that most of it would be another piece I wrote for *Architectural Digest*, entitled "Sky-scraper National Park." But that piece turned out to be so badly written that I am surprised they printed it. What made me garble it so, I think, was my undying fantasy that I would be a contented person if only I could become a member of a Folk Society. That is my Holy Grail, and I can't stop believing, in defiance of all common sense, that it is mine to find somewhere. So this chapter has *filets* cut from the published essay, but they are not set apart by quotation marks, a cumbersome exercise in scholarship. Who cares anyway?)

I spend most of my time in Manhattan, across the street from the yellow house where E. B. White lived for many years. He and his wife Katherine, personifications (you would think) of all that was most cultivated and gracious and witty about Manhattan, bugged out for Maine a few years before I got there. (Maine! Maine? For Pete's sake. Maine!)

It took a foreigner with whom I had no language in common to describe for me the peculiar ambience of Manhattan. He was the great Turkish novelist Yaşar Kemal (who resembles a genuinely happy Ernest Hemingway, although he has been jailed again and again for crimes of conscience). He was in New York

City for the first time, and he and I walked down Broadway from about Sixtieth Street to SoHo, with many side trips to the east and west. I showed him Edna St. Vincent Millay's quaint house. I showed him Washington Square and said, "Henry James! Henry James!" (Just as I had exclaimed to him earlier, "Edna St. Vincent Millay! Edna St. Vincent Millay!" Proper names need no translator, although it is unlikely that Yaşar Kemal had heard of either author.)

I had no idea what the Turk made of it all. But when he got back home (he would soon be back in the hoosegow for the umpteenth time) he wrote me a letter which his translator wife put into English. It said in part, "Suddenly I understood! New York belonged as much to me as to anyone *as long as I was there!*" And there you have the essence of the part of Manhattan I had walked him through, which I in my *Architectural Digest* piece called "Skyscraper National Park."

There are people who go to great lengths to prove that they own some part of Skyscraper National Park, putting their names on buildings or whatever, but they might as well put their names on things like the Grand Canyon or Old Faithful (which will spout at your convenience if you pour a box of laundry detergent down the hole). Manhattan is a geological phenomenon. An enormous fraction of the planet's wealth was concentrated on a little island of solid granite. This caused crystals to sprout in such profusion that the island when viewed from the air now resembles a quartz porcupine.

If I am ever going to find a Folk Society for myself (and time is growing short), it will not be on Manhattan. The members of such a society, Dr. Redfield taught me, must feel that a particular piece of land gave birth to them, and has been and always will be theirs. As I say, nobody can really own anything in Skyscraper National Park.

I have said in speeches that Dr. Redfield, by describing a Folk Society, deserved to be honored alongside the identifiers of vitamins and minerals essential to our good health and cheerfulness. Sailors in the British Navy used to feel lousy on long sea voyages because they weren't getting enough vitamin C. Then they started sucking on limes and they felt OK again. (That is why we call British people limeys. Their sailors were thought to be ridiculous for sucking limes.) I have asserted that a lot of us were wasting away for want of a Folk Society. But vitamins and minerals are real, and Folk Societies, if any survive anywhere, are probably quack remedies for what ails people like me, on the order of Lydia E. Pinkham's Vegetable Compound for Female Complaints.

I visited the Anthropology Department of the University of Chicago a few months ago. Dr. Sol Tax was the only faculty member from my time who was still teaching there. I asked him if he knew what had become of my own classmates (including Lisa Redfield, Dr. Redfield's daughter). Many of them, Lisa, too, he said, were practicing what he called "urban anthropology," which sounded an awful lot like sociology to me. (We used to look down on the sociologists. I couldn't imagine why and can't imagine why.) If I had stayed with anthropology as a career, I would now be doing, probably, what I *am* doing, which is writing about the acculturated primitive people (like myself) in Skyscraper National Park.

A vitamin or mineral deficiency always has bad effects. A Folk Society deficiency (hereafter "FSD") quite often does. The trouble begins when a person suffering from FSD stops thinking, in order to become a member of an artificial extended family which happens to be crazy. The homicidal "family" of Charles Manson springs to mind. Or what about the cult of the Reverend Jim Jones in Guyana, whose members on his advice ("Tonight you will be with me in Paradise") fed the kids Kool-Aid laced with cyanide and then drank it themselves. (The Reverend Jones, like Manson, was from Indianapolis. I didn't tell John Updike that before his lecture there. I had already given him enough information about a city he would probably never see again. Why send him out there with an overload?) And there is the Ku Klux

Klan (whose national headquarters was in Indiana when I was a little boy). And there is the National Rifle Association. And there are all those people who exhibit weirdness if they work in the White House for very long.

Every cockamamie artificial extended family of FSD sufferers resembles Redfield's Folk Society to this extent: it has a myth at its core. The Manson family pretended to believe (the same thing as believing) that its murders would be blamed on blacks. Los Angeles would then be purified somehow by a race war. The myth at the core of the political family which calls itself "Neo-Conservatives" isn't that explicit, but I know what it is, even if most of them can't put it into words. This is it: They are British aristocrats, graduates of Oxford or Cambridge, living in the world as it was one hundred years ago.

Did anyone back then ever look more worn-out by the White Man's Burden than do William F. Buckley, Jr., and our former Representative at the United Nations Jeane Kirkpatrick in the present day? What to do about the Hottentots?

This delusion is in most cases comical. But it has also been tragical for dark-skinned poor people not just in this country but in many, many other parts of the world, since the Neo-Cons have been so influential in shaping our foreign policy during the past ten years. Never mind domestic policy. Foreign policy got all the money.

I mean, my goodness, at one point they had our battleship fire salvos into Lebanon, with no particular targets in mind. That was a scene straight out of Joseph Conrad's *Heart of Darkness*. That book was published way back in 1902, when the idea that upper-class white people were the most highly evolved animals on Earth, and that poor people and dark people were monkeys without tails, had yet to be discredited. The Neo-Cons had our planes fire rockets at monkeys without tails in Tripoli (hitting, among other things, Qaddafi's daughter and the French Embassy). They had us kill maybe one thousand monkeys without tails in the process of arresting one monkey without a tail, the Head of State, in Panama. And there are all these other gruesome things we did or are still doing to monkeys without tails in Guatemala and El Salvador and Nicaragua and the South Bronx and Mozambique, and who knows where else? ("Only the Shadow knows.")

Who but an organ grinder cries when a monkey dies? Not even another monkey.

(Don Quixote was a Neo-Conservative in his time, but all he did was bust a sail on a windmill and scare some sheep.)

XIV

I tried to deal some with the Neo-Cons' wrong-centuryism and wrong-countryism in a novel I finished four months ago, *Hocus Pocus*. The Franklin Library is (at this writing) preparing a deluxe edition of *Hocus Pocus* (with an illustration by my daughter Edith, the former Mrs. Geraldo Rivera, now married to a really great guy) for which I have provided a special preface.

It says that I, ever since studying anthropology, "have regarded history and cultures and societies as characters vivid as any in fiction, as Madame Bovary or Long John Silver or Leopold Bloom or who you will. A critic for *The Village Voice* announced in triumph sometime back his discovery that I was the only well-known writer who had never created a character, and that the next step should be to unfrock me on that account. He was incorrect, since Eliot Rosewater and Billy Pilgrim and some others of my invention are surely stereophonic and three-dimensional, and as idiosyncratic as you please. But he was onto something nonetheless: In many of my books, including this one, individual human beings are not the main characters.

"The biggest character in *Hocus Pocus* (excluding myself, of course) is imperialism, the capture of other societies' lands and people and treasure by means of state-of-the-art wounding and killing machines, which is to say armies and navies. It can't be said too often that when Christopher Columbus discovered this hemisphere there were already millions upon millions of human beings here, and heavily armed Europeans took it away from them. When executed on a smaller scale, such an enterprise is the felony we call armed robbery. As might be expected, violence of this sort has not been without its consequences, one of which turns out to be the unwillingness of the richest heirs of the conquerors to take responsibility for what has become an awful lot of complicated property in need of skilled management and exceedingly boring and appallingly expensive maintenance, not to mention an increasingly unhappy and destructive and ailing general population.

"But in *Hocus Pocus,* as in real life this very minute, the richest heirs in what has become the United States have been rescued by foreigners, most famously cash-heavy Japanese, eager to buy the country with paper forms of wealth negotiable almost anywhere and free of the least implication of social or managerial obligations. Heaven! So those heirs, many of whom captured the fruits of the European conquest of this part of the Western Hemisphere only recently, through activities in bad faith on Wall Street or the looting of savings banks, reveal themselves as being no more patriotic about where they live than were the British conquerors of Rhodesia, the Belgian conquerors of the Congo, or the Portuguese conquerors of Mozambique. Or all the different sorts of foreigners who are buying up the USA."

There was more to that preface, but the heck with it. (The older I get, the less willing I am to stand behind anything I say or do. Then again, all I do is louse up paper, whereas Ronald Reagan, who used to work for General Electric, too, loused up the whole country. GE itself, of course, loused up the Hudson

River and several hundred square miles downwind from Hanford, Washington.)

What I wish I'd said in the preface (senile *esprit de l'escalier*) is that we are the last big colony to be abandoned by its conquerors. After they are gone, taking most of our money with them (maybe to Europe, maybe to compounds right here in the former colony, such as the Hamptons or Palm Beach or Palm Springs), we will be like Nigeria, a sort of improbable Dr. Seuss–type nation composed of several tribes. In Nigeria (which I visited during a tribal war) the biggest tribes are the Hausas, the Yorubas, and the Ibos. Here they will be the Blacks, the Hispanics, the Irish, the Italians, the Asiatics, and the Nothings (which would include those of German descent).

There will be clashes. We will be a Third World country. The only consolation is that every other country will be Third World, too. (You watch!) Thanks to the inevitable aftereffects of imperialism, of taking people's land away and busting up their cultures, this will be a Third World planet.

I proposed this theory to Salman Rushdie, who has said that Britain itself is the last outpost of Empire, having imported dark-skinned former subjects for mistreatment right there on the island where it all began. Rushdie, whom I mentioned in my piece about Nelson Algren, is in hiding, having had a contract put out on him by Iran. So I wrote him a letter. There has been no reply so far, but he *did* publish a killer of a review of *Hocus Pocus* in a British paper, saying that I was a burned-out case and so on. (I was so upset I considered putting a contract out on him.)

Things are bad. (The best book I ever wrote was *Galápagos*, in which I said that our big brains were making our lives unbearable.) The most trusted man in America is said to be Walter Cronkite. (Who else is there?) He used to be my friend, but now he is very cold to me. Imagine being an American and being treated like something the cat drug in by the most trusted man in America! (Imagine being an American.)

Further on in the preface I went after American Eastern Seaboard prep schools again. (I am bughouse on that subject.) I said that those schools were clones of British prep schools, and that their idea of character was the so-called "muscular Christianity" exhibited by aristocratic imperialists in the time of Queen Victoria. (Those old-timers sure knew how to deal with monkeys without tails.) And then along comes *Masterpiece Theatre* on so-called "Public Television," dramatizing stories about the beauty and charm and wittiness not only of British imperialism but of the British class system as well. The British class system is as subversive of what the United States once hoped to be and might have been and should have been as *Das Kapital* or *Mein Kampf*. (Why is it, do you suppose, that the lower social orders don't watch more Public TV?)

British imperialism was armed robbery. The British class system (which seems so right to the Neo-Cons) was and still is unarmed robbery. (Just because the Soviet Union, which used to brag about being such a friend of the common people, has collapsed, that doesn't mean the Sermon on the Mount must now be considered balderdash.)

I try to be fair. I have been wrong in the past, and could be wrong again, blaming prep schools and *Masterpiece Theatre* for the status quo. (During the Great Depression, my unicorn father's favorite radio show was *Amos 'n' Andy,* which took white people's minds off their troubles by making light of the troubles of black people. I remember one elegant joke from that show. It was a pretend black man's, actually a white man's, definition of *status quo* as "de mess we's in.") It could be that we's in de mess we's in because we's plain done went bananas. I dealt with that in an essay published in *The Nation* (read by one American in every twenty-five hundred). It went like this:

"What has been America's most nurturing contribution to the culture of this planet so far? Many would say jazz. I, who love jazz, will say this instead: Alcoholics Anonymous.

"I am not an alcoholic. If I were, I would go before the nearest

AA meeting and say, 'My name is Kurt Vonnegut. I am an alcoholic.' God willing, that might be my first step down the long, hard road back to sobriety.

"The AA scheme, which requires a confession like that, is the first to have any measurable success in dealing with the tendency of some human beings, perhaps ten percent of any population sample anyone might care to choose, to become addicted to substances that give them brief spasms of pleasure but in the long term transmute their lives and the lives of those around them into ultimate ghastliness.

"The AA scheme, which, again, can work only if the addicts regularly admit that this or that chemical is poisonous to them, is now proving its effectiveness with compulsive gamblers, who are not dependent on chemicals from a distillery or a pharmaceutical laboratory. This is no paradox. Gamblers, in effect, manufacture their own dangerous substances. God help them, they produce chemicals that elate them whenever they place a bet on simply anything.

"If I were a compulsive gambler, which I am not, I would be well advised to stand up before the nearest meeting of Gamblers Anonymous and declare, 'My name is Kurt Vonnegut. I am a compulsive gambler.'

"Whether the meeting I was standing before was of Gamblers Anonymous or Alcoholics Anonymous, I would be encouraged to testify as to how the chemicals I had generated within myself or swallowed had alienated my friends and relatives, cost me jobs and houses, and deprived me of my last shred of self-respect.

"Not every member of AA or GA has sunk quite that low, of course—but plenty have. Many, if not most, have done what they call 'hitting bottom' before admitting what it is that has been ruining their lives.

"I now wish to direct your attention to another form of addiction, which has not been previously identified. It is more like gambling than drinking, since the people afflicted are ravenous for situations that will cause their bodies to release exciting chemicals into their bloodstreams. I am persuaded that there are among us people who are tragically hooked on preparations for war.

"Tell people with that disease that war is coming and we have to get ready for it, and for a few minutes there, they will be as happy as a drunk with his martini breakfast or a compulsive gambler with his paycheck bet on the Super Bowl.

"Let us recognize how sick such people are. From now on, when a national leader, or even just a neighbor, starts talking about some new weapons system which is going to cost us a mere $29 billion, we should speak up. We should say something on the order of, 'Honest to God, I couldn't be sorrier for you if I'd seen you wash down a fistful of black beauties with a pint of Southern Comfort.'

"I mean it. I am not joking. Compulsive preparers for World War III, in this country or any other, are as tragically and, yes, as repulsively addicted as any stockbroker passed out with his head in a toilet in Port Authority Bus Terminal.

"For an alcoholic to experience a little joy, he needs maybe three ounces of grain alcohol. Alcoholics, when they are close to hitting bottom, customarily can't hold much alcohol.

"If we know a compulsive gambler who is dead broke, we can probably make him happy with a dollar to bet on who can spit farther than someone else.

"For us to give a compulsive war-preparer a fleeting moment of happiness, we may have to buy him three Trident submarines and a hundred intercontinental ballistic missiles mounted on choo-choo trains.

"If Western Civilization were a person—

"If Western Civilization, which blankets the world now, as far as I can tell, were a person—

"If Western Civilization, which surely now includes the Soviet Union and China and India and Pakistan and on and on, were a person—

"If Western Civilization were a person, we would be directing it to the nearest meeting of War Preparers Anonymous. We would be telling it to stand up before the meeting and say, 'My name is Western Civilization. I am a compulsive war-preparer. I have lost everything I ever cared about. I should have come here long ago. I first hit bottom in World War I.'

"Western Civilization cannot be represented by a single person, of course, but a single explanation for the catastrophic course it has followed during this bloody century is possible. We the people, because of our ignorance of the disease, have again and again entrusted power to people we did not know were sickies.

"And let us not mock them now, any more than we would mock someone with syphilis or smallpox or leprosy or yaws or typhoid fever or any of the other diseases to which the flesh is heir. All we have to do is separate them from the levers of power, I think.

"And then what?

"Western Civilization's long, hard trip back to sobriety might begin.

"A word about appeasement, something World War II, supposedly, taught us not to practice: I say to you that the world has been ruined by appeasement. Appeasement of whom? Of the Communists? Of the Neo-Nazis? No! Appeasement of the compulsive war-preparers. I can scarcely name a nation that has not lost most of its freedom and wealth in attempts to appease its own addicts to preparations for war.

"And there is no appeasing an addict for very long: 'I swear, man, just lay enough bread on me for twenty multiple-reentry vehicles and a fleet of B-1 bombers, and I'll never bother you again.'

"Most addictions start innocently enough in childhood, under agreeable, reputable auspices—a sip of champagne at a wedding, a game of poker for matchsticks on a rainy afternoon.

Compulsive war-preparers may have been encouraged as infants to clap their hands with glee at a campfire or a Fourth of July parade.

"Not every child gets hooked. Not every child so tempted grows up to be a drunk or a gambler or a babbler about knocking down the incoming missiles of the Evil Empire with laser beams. When I identify the war preparers as addicts, I am not calling for the exclusion of children from all martial celebrations. I doubt that more than one child in a hundred, having seen fireworks, for example, will become an adult who wants us to stop squandering our substance on education and health and social justice and the arts, and food and shelter and clothing for the needy, and so on—who wants us to blow it all on ammunition instead.

"And please understand that the addiction I have identified is to *preparations* for war. I repeat: to *preparations* for war—addiction to the thrills of de-mothballing battleships and inventing weapons systems against which there cannot possibly be a defense, supposedly, and urging the citizenry to hate this part of humanity or that one, and knocking over little governments that might aid and abet an enemy someday, and so on. I am not talking about an addiction to war itself, which is a very different matter. A compulsive preparer for war no more wants to go to big-time war than an alcoholic stockbroker wants to pass out with his head in a toilet in Port Authority Bus Terminal.

"Should addicts of any sort hold high offices in this or any other country? Absolutely not, for their first priority will always be to satisfy their addiction, no matter how terrible the consequences may be—even to themselves.

"Suppose we had an alcoholic President who still had not hit bottom and whose chief companions were drunks like himself. And suppose it were a fact, made absolutely clear to him, that if he took just one more drink, the whole planet would blow up.

"He has all the liquor thrown out of the White House, including his Aqua Velva shaving lotion. Late at night he is terribly restless, crazy for a drink but proud of not drinking. So he opens the White House refrigerator, looking for a Tab or a Diet Pepsi, he tells himself. And there, half hidden by a family-size jar of French's mustard, is an unopened can of Coors beer.

"What do you think he'll do?"

I wrote that seven years ago, and have used it in speeches many times since. (Even Jesus Christ, if He hadn't been crucified, would have started repeating Himself.) It could be classed as a practical joke, since I was only pretending to be serious. (Then again, all wordplay or fiction or speeches or whatever is practical joking, since people are made to feel fear or love or satisfaction or whatever while they are simply sitting someplace and nothing much is really going on.)

The best practical joke I ever heard of (and it may have been Hugh Troy's doing) involved a man in an ad agency who got a big promotion and went out and bought a homburg hat as a badge of rank. Some people in the office pooled their money to buy several identical homburgs, but of different sizes, which they substituted from time to time for the one the man had bought for himself. So when the man went out to lunch or whatever and put on his hat, it had to seem to him that his head was swelling or shrinking, since sometimes the hat sat way up high (like a gumdrop), and sometimes it came down over his eyes and ears (like a diving bell).

I used to say that the funniest word joke in the world was the one which asked, "Why is cream more expensive than milk?" Answer: "Because the cows hate to squat on those little bottles." Technological changes in the dairy industry require me to take away the joke's championship. Cream is no longer sold in glass bottles with wide mouths over which a cow might conceivably be forced to squat. So the new champion is an oldie from the golden age of radio comedy, during which Ed Wynn ("The Perfect Fool") was cast as a Fire Chief. Each show began with

Wynn's conducting some sort of ridiculous Fire Department business on the telephone. One time a woman called up to say her house was on fire. Wynn asked her if she had tried putting water on it. She said she had, and he said, "I'm sorry, but that's all we could do." He hung up.

(So there's the new World's Champion.)

XV

And get a load of this naive sermon I preached at the Cathedral
of St. John the Divine in New York City:

"I will speak today about the worst imaginable consequences
of doing without hydrogen bombs. This should be a relief. I am
sure you are sick and tired of hearing how all living things sizzle
and pop inside a radioactive fireball. We have known that for
more than a third of this century—ever since we dropped an
atom bomb on the yellow people of Hiroshima. *They* certainly
sizzled and popped.

"After all is said and done, what was that sizzling and popping, despite the brilliant technology which caused it, but our
old friend death? Let us not forget that St. Joan of Arc was
made to sizzle and pop in old times with nothing more than
firewood. She wound up dead. The people of Hiroshima wound
up dead. Dead is dead.

"Scientists, for all their creativity, will never discover a
method for making people deader than dead. So if some of you
are worried about being hydrogen-bombed, you are merely fear-

ing death. There is nothing new in that. If there weren't any hydrogen bombs, death would still be after you. And what is death but an absence of life? That is all it ever can be.

"Death is nothing. What is all this fuss about?

"Let us 'up the ante,' as gamblers say. Let us talk about fates *worse* than death. When the Reverend Jim Jones saw that his followers in Guyana were facing fates worse than death, he gave them Kool-Aid laced with cyanide. If our government sees that we are facing fates worse than death, it will shower our enemies with hydrogen bombs, and then we will be showered in turn. There will be plenty of Kool-Aid for everyone, in a manner of speaking, when the right time comes.

"What will the right time look like?

"I will not waste your time with trivial fates, which are only marginally worse than death. Suppose we were conquered by an enemy, for example, who didn't understand our wonderful economic system, and so Braniff airlines and International Harvester and so on all went bust, and millions of Americans who wanted to work couldn't find any jobs anywhere. Or suppose we were conquered by an enemy who was too cheap to take good care of children and old people. Or suppose we were conquered by an enemy who wouldn't spend money on anything but weapons for World War III. These are all tribulations we could live with, if we had to—although God forbid.

"But suppose we foolishly got rid of our nuclear weapons, our Kool-Aid, and an enemy came over here and crucified us. Crucifixion was the most painful thing the ancient Romans ever found to do to anyone. They knew as much about pain as we do about genocide. They sometimes crucified hundreds of people at one time. That is what they did to all the survivors of the army of Spartacus, which was composed mostly of escaped slaves. They crucified them all. There were several miles of crosses.

"If we were up on crosses, with nails through our feet and

hands, wouldn't we wish that we still had hydrogen bombs, so that life could be ended everywhere? Absolutely.

"We know of one person who was crucified in olden times, who was supposedly as capable as we or the Russians are of ending life everywhere. But He chose to endure agony instead. All He said was, 'Forgive them, Father—they know not what they do.'

"He let life go on, as awful as it was for Him, because here we are, aren't we?

"But He was a special case. It is unfair to use Jesus Christ as an exemplar of how much pain and humiliation we ordinary human beings should put up with before calling for the end of everything.

"I don't believe that we *are* about to be crucified. No potential enemy we now face has anywhere near enough carpenters. Not even people at the Pentagon at budget time have mentioned crucifixion. I am sorry to have to put that idea into their heads. I will have only myself to blame if, a year from now, the Joint Chiefs of Staff testify under oath that we are on the brink of being crucified.

"But what if they said, instead, that we would be enslaved if we did not appropriate enough money for weaponry? That could be true. Despite our worldwide reputation for sloppy workmanship, wouldn't some enemy get a kick out of forcing us into involuntary servitude, buying and selling us like so many household appliances or farm machines or inflatable erotic toys?

"And slavery would surely be a fate worse than death. We can agree on that, I'm sure. We should send a message to the Pentagon: 'If Americans are about to become enslaved, it is Kool-Aid time.'

"They will know what we mean.

"Of course, at Kool-Aid time all higher forms of life on Earth, not just we and our enemies, will be killed. Even those beautiful and fearless and utterly stupid seabirds the defenseless blue-footed boobies of the Galápagos Islands will die, because we object to slavery.

"I have seen those birds, by the way—up close. I could have unscrewed their heads, if I had wanted to. I made a trip to the Galápagos Islands two months ago—in the company of, among other people, Paul Moore, Jr., the bishop of this very cathedral.

"That is the sort of company I keep these days—everything from bishops to blue-footed boobies. I have never seen a human slave, though. But my four great-grandfathers saw slaves. When they came to this country in search of justice and opportunity, there were millions of Americans who were slaves. The equation which links a strong defense posture to not being enslaved is laid down in that stirring fight song, much heard lately, 'Rule, Britannia.' I will sing the equation:

" 'Rule, Britannia; Britannia, rule the waves—'

"That, of course, is a poetic demand for a Navy second to none. I now sing the next line, which explains why it is essential to have a Navy that good:

" 'Britons never, never, never shall be slaves.'

"It may surprise some of you to learn what an old equation that is. The Scottish poet who wrote it, James Thomson, died in 1748—about a quarter of a century before there was such a country as the United States of America. Thomson promised Britons that they would never be slaves, at a time when the enslavement of persons with inferior weaponry was a respectable industry. Plenty of people were going to be slaves, and it would serve them right, too—but Britons would not be among them.

"So that isn't really a very nice song. It is about not being humiliated, which is all right. But it is also about humiliating others, which is not a moral thing to do. The humiliation of others should never be a national goal.

"There is one poet who should have been ashamed of himself.

"If the Soviet Union came over here and enslaved us, it wouldn't be the first time Americans were slaves. If we conquered the Russians and enslaved them, it wouldn't be the first time Russians were slaves.

"And the last time Americans were slaves, and the last time Russians were slaves, they displayed astonishing spiritual strengths and resourcefulness. They were good at loving one another. They trusted God. They discovered in the simplest, most natural satisfactions reasons to be glad to be alive. They were able to believe that better days were coming in the sweet by-and-by. And here is a fascinating statistic: They committed suicide less often than their masters did.

"So Americans and Russians can both stand slavery, if they have to—and still want life to go on and on.

"Could it be that slavery *isn't* a fate worse than death? After all, people are tough. Maybe we shouldn't send that message to the Pentagon—about slavery and Kool-Aid time.

"But suppose enemies came ashore in great numbers because we lacked the means to stop them, and they pushed us out of our homes and off our ancestral lands, and into swamps and deserts. Suppose that they even tried to destroy our religion, telling us that our Great God Jehovah, or whatever we wanted to call Him, was as ridiculous as a piece of junk jewelry.

"Again: This is a wringer millions of Americans have already been through—or are still going through. It is another catastrophe Americans can endure, if they have to—still, miraculously, maintaining some measure of dignity, or self-respect.

"As bad as life is for our Indians, they still like it better than death.

"So I haven't had much luck, have I, in identifying fates worse than death? Crucifixion is the only clear winner so far, and we aren't about to be crucified. We aren't about to be enslaved, either—to be treated the way white Americans used to treat black Americans. And no potential enemy that I have heard of wants to come over here to treat all of us the way we still treat American Indians.

"What other fates worse than death could I name? Life without petroleum?

"In melodramas of a century ago, a female's loss of virginity outside of holy wedlock was sometimes spoken of as a fate worse than death. I hope that isn't what the Pentagon or the Kremlin has in mind—but you never know.

"I would rather die for virginity than for petroleum, I think. It's more literary, somehow.

"I may be blinding myself to the racist aspects of hydrogen bombs, whose only function is to end everything. Perhaps there are tribulations that *white* people should not be asked to tolerate. But the Russians' slaves were white. The supposedly unenslavable Britons were enslaved by the Romans. Even proud Britons, if they were enslaved now, would have to say, 'Here we go again.' Armenians and Jews have certainly been treated hideously in modern as well as ancient times—and they have still wanted life to go on and on and on. About a third of our own white people were robbed and ruined and scorned after our Civil War. They still wanted life to go on and on and on.

"Have there ever been large numbers of human beings of any sort who have not, despite everything, done all they could to keep life going on and on and on?

"Soldiers.

" 'Death before dishonor' was the motto of several military formations during the Civil War—on both sides. It may be the motto of the 82nd Airborne Division right now. A motto like that made a certain amount of sense, I suppose, when military death was what happened to the soldier on the right or the left of you—or in front of you, or in back of you. But military death now can easily mean the death of everything, including, as I have already said, the blue-footed boobies of the Galápagos Islands.

"The webbed feet of those birds really are the brightest blue, by the way. When two blue-footed boobies begin a courtship, they show each other what beautiful bright blue feet they have.

"If you go to the Galápagos Islands, and see all the strange creatures, you are bound to think what Charles Darwin thought when he went there: How much time Nature has in which to accomplish simply anything. If we desolate this planet, Nature can get life going again. All it takes is a few million years or so, the wink of an eye to Nature.

"Only humankind is running out of time.

"My guess is that we will not disarm, even though we should, and that we really will blow up everything by and by. History shows that human beings are vicious enough to commit every imaginable atrocity, including the construction of factories whose only purpose is to kill people and burn them up.

"It may be that we were put here on Earth to blow the place to smithereens. We may be Nature's way of creating new galaxies. We may be programmed to improve and improve our weapons, and to believe that death is better than dishonor.

"And then, one day, as disarmament rallies are being held all over the planet, *ka-blooey!* A new Milky Way is born.

"Perhaps we should be adoring instead of loathing our hydrogen bombs. They could be the eggs for new galaxies.

"What can save us? Divine intervention, certainly—and this is the place to ask for it. We might pray to be rescued from our inventiveness, just as the dinosaurs may have prayed to be rescued from their massiveness.

"But the inventiveness which we so regret now may also be giving us, along with the rockets and warheads, the means to achieve what has hitherto been an impossibility, the unity of mankind. I am talking mainly about television sets.

"Even in my own lifetime, it used to be necessary for a young soldier to get into fighting before he became disillusioned about war. His parents back home were equally ignorant, and believed him to be slaying monsters. But now, thanks to modern communications, the people of every industrialized nation are nauseated by the idea of war by the time they are ten years old. America's first generation of television viewers has gone to war and come home again—and we have never seen veterans like them before.

"What makes the Vietnam veterans so somehow spooky? We could describe them almost as being 'unwholesomely mature.' They have *never* had illusions about war. They are the first soldiers in history who knew even in childhood, from having heard and seen so many pictures of actual and restaged battles, that war is meaningless butchery of ordinary people like themselves.

"It used to be that veterans could shock their parents when they came home, as Ernest Hemingway did, by announcing that everything about war was repulsive and stupid and dehumanizing. But the parents of our Vietnam veterans were disillusioned about war, too, many of them having seen it firsthand before their children went overseas. Thanks to modern communications, Americans of all ages were dead sick of war even before we went into Vietnam.

"Thanks to modern communications, the poor, unlucky young people from the Soviet Union, now killing and dying in Afghanistan, were dead sick of war before they ever got there.

"Thanks to modern communications, the same must be true of the poor, unlucky young people from Argentina and Great Britain, now killing and dying in the Falkland Islands. The *New York Post* calls them 'Argies' and 'Brits.' Thanks to modern communications, we know that they are a good deal more marvelous and complicated than that, and that what is happening to them down there, on the rim of the Antarctic, is a lot more horrible and shameful than a soccer match.

"When I was a boy it was unusual for an American, or a person of any nationality for that matter, to know much about foreigners. Those who did were specialists—diplomats, explorers, journalists, anthropologists. And they usually knew a lot about just a few groups of foreigners, Eskimos maybe, or Arabs, or what have you. To them, as to the schoolchildren of Indianapolis, large areas of the globe were terra incognita.

"Now look what has happened. Thanks to modern communications, we have seen sights and heard sounds from virtually every square mile of landmass on this planet. Millions of us have actually visited more exotic places than had explorers during my childhood. Many of you have been to Timbuktu. Many of you have been to Katmandu. My dentist just got home from Fiji. He told me all about Fiji. If he had taken his fingers out of my mouth, I would have told him about the Galápagos Islands.

"So we now know for *certain* that there are no potential human enemies anywhere who are anything but human beings almost exactly like ourselves. They need food. How amazing. They love their children. How amazing. They obey their leaders. How amazing. They think like their neighbors. How amazing.

"Thanks to modern communications, we now have something we never had before: reason to mourn deeply the death or wounding of any human being on any side in any war.

"It was because of rotten communications and malicious, racist ignorance that we were able to celebrate the killing of almost all the inhabitants in Hiroshima, Japan, thirty-seven years ago. We thought they were vermin. They thought we were vermin. They would have clapped their little yellow hands with glee and grinned with their crooked buckteeth if they could have incinerated everybody in Kansas City, say.

"Thanks to how much the people of the world now know about all the other people of the world, the fun of killing enemies has lost its zing. It has so lost its zing that no sane citizen of the Soviet Union, if we were to go to war with that society, would feel anything but horror if his country were to kill practically everybody in New York and Chicago and San Francisco. Killing enemies has so lost its zing that no sane citizen of the United States would feel anything but horror if our country were to kill practically everybody in Moscow and Leningrad and Kiev.

"Or in Nagasaki, Japan, for that matter.

"We have often heard it said that people would have to change, or we would go on having world wars. I bring you good news this morning: People have changed.

"We aren't so ignorant and bloodthirsty anymore.

"I dreamed last night of our descendants a thousand years from now, which is to say all of humanity. If you're at all into reproduction, as was the Emperor Charlemagne, you can pick up an awful lot of relatives in a thousand years. Every person in this cathedral who has a drop of white blood is a descendant of Charlemagne.

"A thousand years from now, if there are still human beings on Earth, every one of those human beings will be descended from us—and from everyone who has chosen to reproduce.

"In my dream, our descendants are numerous. Some of them are rich, some are poor, some are likable, some are insufferable.

"I ask them how humanity, against all odds, managed to keep going for another millennium. They tell me that they and their ancestors did it by preferring life over death for themselves and others at every opportunity, even at the expense of being dishonored. They endured all sorts of insults and humiliations and disappointments without committing either suicide or murder. They are also the people who do the insulting and humiliating and disappointing.

"I endear myself to them by suggesting a motto they might like to put on their belt buckles or T-shirts or whatever. They aren't all hippies, by the way. They aren't all Americans, either. They aren't even all white people.

"I give them a quotation from that great nineteenth-century moralist and robber baron, Jim Fisk, who may have contributed money to this cathedral.

"Jim Fisk uttered his famous words after a particularly disgraceful episode having to do with the Erie Railroad. Fisk himself had no choice but to find himself contemptible. He thought this over, and then he shrugged and said what we all must learn to say if we want to go on living much longer: 'Nothing is lost save honor.'

"I thank you for your attention."

Here is how I happened to have the use of the high pulpit and public-address system of the Cathedral of St. John the Divine (the biggest Gothic church in the world): The management invited several persons famously opposed to nuclear weaponry to preach on sequential Sundays in the spring of 1983. I was one of those, and I must have blown a gasket while solemnly mounting the pulpit stairs. Why do I say that? I was so blitheringly optimistic! I was like a hack politician, saying what I thought would most please a particular audience, Lithuanian-Americans, leather workers, Daughters of the American Revolution, or whatever. My narrowly specialized audience was a gathering of war-haters on the edge of an enormously rich nation whose most fascinating projects and popular entertainments had to do with war, war, war.

Three-quarters of my speech was truthful. But then came this whopper: That TV was a pacifier. If I had been in the congregation, and some other preacher had said that, I would have walked right out of that cathedral and slammed the two-ton door behind me. American TV, operating in the Free Market of Ideas (which I have said elsewhere is so good for us), was holding audiences with simulations of one of the two things most human beings, and especially young ones, can't help watching when given the opportunity: murder. TV, and of course movies, too, were and still are making us as callous about killing and death as Hitler's propaganda made the German people during the frenzied prelude to the death camps and World War II.

Who needs a Joseph Goebbels to make us think killing is as quotidian an activity as tying one's shoes? All that is needed is a TV industry which is self-supporting, which can't make enough money to survive unless it gets a great big audience.

What I should have said from the pulpit was that we weren't *going* to Hell. We were *in* Hell, thanks to technology which was telling us what to do, instead of the other way around. And it wasn't just TV. It was weapons which could actually kill everything half a world away. It was vehicles powered by glurp from underground which could make a fat old lady go a mile a minute while picking her nose and listening to the radio. And so on. (In what spiritual detail, I should have asked, did the glurp-powered automobile or Harley-Davidson differ from freebased cocaine? And was there anything we wouldn't do to ensure that the glurp kept on coming? And were we all going to go positively apeshit when there was no more glurp?)

On the subject of how casual technology had made us about war, I should have called attention to the transmogrification of my birthday, November 11, from Armistice Day to Veterans Day. When I was a boy, all human activity in Indianapolis (except for fucking, I suppose) stopped for one minute. That was the eleventh minute of the eleventh hour of the eleventh day of the eleventh month. It was during that same minute back in 1918 when World War I stopped. (It wouldn't start up again until 1939, when the Germans invaded Poland, or maybe in 1931, when the Japanese occupied Manchuria. What a mess!) On Armistice Day, children used to be told how horrible war was, how shameful and heartbreaking, which was right. The proper way to commemorate any war would be to paint ourselves blue and roll in the mud and grunt like pigs.

But in 1945, Armistice Day became Veterans Day, and by the time I was preaching in St. John's, the message of November 11 was that there were going to be lots more wars, and that we were ready for them this time (were we ever!), and that not just boys but girls, too, should want to grow up to be veterans (don't be left out!).

We hadn't yet killed more than a thousand Panamanians in the process of kidnapping their Head of State (a paid CIA agent) on suspicion of drug trafficking, or I sure would have talked about that. I would have reminded people my age what Captain J. W. Philip said to his crewmen aboard the Battleship *Texas* in Santiago Bay in 1898 during the Spanish-American War. (American public school kids used to know his words by heart. I bet they don't anymore.) Shellfire from the *Texas* had set the Spanish Cruiser *Vizcaya* ablaze from stem to stern. And Captain Philip said, "Don't cheer, boys, those poor devils are dying." War back then, while perhaps necessary and surely exciting, was also a tragedy. It is still a tragedy, and can never be otherwise. But while we were zapping Panamanians all I heard from the top of our power structure were variations on "whee" and "whoopee."

(Yes, and while I was doing the final editing on this book, which was written in the summer of 1990 and is supposed to be about the 1980s, we experienced our great victory over Iraq. I will simply repeat what a woman said at supper a week after we stopped shooting and bombing and rocketing: "The atmosphere of this country now is like a big party in a beautiful home. Everybody is polite and bubbly, but there is this awful stink coming from somewhere, and it's getting worse and worse. And nobody wants to be the first to mention it.")

The only warfare Ronald Reagan ever saw was in the movies, of course. Everybody was glad to be fighting. Wounds were never messy and wounded people were never noisy, and nobody died in vain. And George Bush was a war hero of the first rank, beyond doubt. But he was an aviator, so war must have felt like a sport, one hell of a scary sport. Aviators almost never have to take a close look at the faces (if any) of people they've killed or wounded. It is common for combat veterans who fought on the ground to have bad dreams about people they killed. Fortunately for me, I never killed anyone. Imagine how ashamed a bombardier or fighter pilot would be if he had to make the same confession, that he hadn't killed anyone.

And then there's the business of George Bush being the first President in my lifetime to be elected after a campaign which was nakedly racist, using a black psychopath as a boogeyman. If he had done that with an Armenian or a Pole or a Jew, he would have been as despicable as Nazidom's Heinrich Himmler, the former chicken farmer who was boss of all the death camps. But Bush knew the United States better than I have ever dared to know them, and he scared us with a black man, and he won, he won. But the heck with that. Blah blah blah. In 1935, Sinclair Lewis published a work of imagination about this country turning Fascist, *It Can't Happen Here.* That's what I say, too: It can't happen here, unless there's another Great Depression, of course.

I was already friends with the Cathedral's bishop, Paul Moore, Jr. Jill had known him since she was a little girl in Morristown, New Jersey. He and his wife Brenda and Jill and I had gone to the Galápagos Islands together. One night when we were right on the Equator (Ecuador!), I asked him to point out a constellation I had never seen, the Southern Cross. He had seen it, I knew, because he had fought as a Marine well south of the Equator, in Guadalcanal. (That was where he got religion. If I had had one, I would have lost it there.) The Southern Cross was a teeny-weeny thing, not much bigger than the head of a thumbtack from our vantage point.

"Sorry," he said.

"Not your fault," I said.

He had lived and preached in Indianapolis for quite a while, and so knew several of my relatives who had backslid into Christianity. He is a very good man, always on the side of the powerless when they are abused or scorned or cheated by the powerful (mostly subscribers to *The Wall Street Journal*). A pregnant woman asked me one time if I thought it was wrong to bring a child into such an awful world. I replied that what made living almost worthwhile for me was all the saints I met, and I named Bishop Moore.

XVI

My first wife, Jane Marie, née Cox, whom I met in kindergarten, was born a Quaker and (as Mrs. Adam Yarmolinsky) died a high Episcopalian. Her Quaker father and brother both served in the Marines. This military variety of Quaker (Richard M. Nixon is a famous example) came into being, I have been told, when Quaker families moved westward in the company of other religious denominations. The children were attracted (as though by carnivals) to services so unlike their own, with music and exciting preachers, and with fantastic battles between God and the Devil to hear about. So the Quaker elders, in order to keep the children Quakers, went into show business, too, and began to talk and think like the more colorful majority. (Result: Richard M. Nixon and my first father-in-law and brother-in-law.)

My first brother-in-law had a nervous crack-up during Marine basic training, but I don't believe that had anything to do with his being a Quaker, not the sort of Quaker *he* was. He was an excellent skater and was invited to join an ice show after he graduated from Indiana University. But his Quaker father sternly opposed that move. So he enlisted in the Marines, where, as I've said, he went bananas. In any case he's OK now. (All's well that ends well.)

My dear Jane went to Swarthmore, a Quaker college near Philadelphia, and expressed love for the austere Quakerism still practiced there, without music or calculated passion, and without preachers. Attendees at Meetings in bare rooms spoke about this or that on the spur of the moment, without any agenda about who was to speak or what the subject should be. Sometimes nobody spoke, she said (e.g., after the bombing of Pearl Harbor). But that, too, was wonderful, perhaps the most moving performance of all, or so Jane said.

But Jane never went to a Quaker Meeting after we were married, although she always made it a first order of business to find out where the nearest one was whenever we took up residence in a new community. She didn't go to Meetings, I think, because Quaker congregations in the East (and we had become easterners) were so close to being Folk Societies as described by Robert Redfield. They were united by blood ties and inhabited a territory which had been theirs for several generations. And here was what was so daunting to Jane or anybody else who might want to join them: They did not welcome strangers, save as well-behaved visitors who would soon have the good manners to go away again. (They were like Israeli youngsters raised on kibbutzim as described in *The Children of the Dream* by Bruno Bettelheim.)

(I was similarly frosted when I was an invited speaker at the Unitarian church on Harvard Square in Cambridge, Massachusetts. I wasn't to consider myself a relative of any sort, and it was obvious that I could not tell that cold-roast professorial bunch anything that it hadn't accepted or dismissed collectively years and years ago. It was like an old kibbutz.)

An early expression of Jane's powerful longing for a big like-minded family was a persistent prediction she began to make in her early teens, that she would one day have seven children.

This came true. We had three of our own, and thought we had
stopped there. But then my sister and her husband died, and we
took in their three kids.

(It makes me think we don't know anything about time when
somebody turns out to have predicted something so complex
and specific so accurately. The sinking of the great ship *Titanic*
was also foreseen. A novelist wrote about it before the ship was
launched.)

Jane did not like the family she came from (partly because
her mother went insane periodically), but she sure adored her
kids, and they adored her. (After our marriage broke up, and
there was a lot of hydrofluoric acid eating holes in my clothing,
so to speak, I told a psychiatrist at a party that my next mate,
if there was to be another one, would have to be a woman who
really loved her mother a lot. The psychiatrist replied that that
was one of the dumbest, most self-destructive things he had ever
heard from the lips of any male or female. "Instead, why don't
you go over Niagara Falls in a barrel?" he said.)

When Jane's beloved children became grownups and flew the
coop one by one, she was again attacked by a terrible loneliness
which I (only one person, and a chain-smoker at that) surely
couldn't begin to satisfy.

So she went in for Transcendental Meditation (TM) with what
seemed to me total abandon. One contemporary of our grown
kids, Jody Clarke, went to work for Maharishi Mahesh Yogi
as a TM recruiter and instructor. He had meditated for thousands of hours (and would be killed in the crash of an airplane
while looking for a good location for a TM ashram in North
Carolina). When Jane told Jody all the glorious things she saw
when she meditated, he was astonished. He said, "My goodness,
I never saw anything like *that!*"

For almost everybody but Jane, TM was blank, brightly lit,
air-conditioned, keenly alert peacefulness. For her it was like
going to the movies. So was Holy Communion, I think, when
she became an Episcopalian. (I doubt that the Pope or Bishop

Paul Moore, Jr., or the battle-axe who wouldn't let Jill and me get married in The Little Church Around the Corner ever came as close to Christ as Jane did with a wafer and wine.) Like her mother, and like her son Mark, too, before he recovered, she was a hallucinator. (Unlike Mark and me, though, she never had to be locked up somewhere.) TM and then Episcopalianism made her visions not only reputable and unfrightening, but holy and fun. (There must be uncounted millions like her, so rapt in churches and concert halls, or on park benches on sunny days with a carousel playing not far away.)

My late war buddy O'Hare was born a Roman Catholic in Pennsylvania but came home from the war a religious skeptic. Bishop Moore, as I've said, went to war a religious skeptic and came out of it a profoundly convinced Trinitarian. He told me he had a vision during the fighting on Guadalcanal. He went on from his vision (although he was born rich and had a rich Anglo-Saxon's education and tastes and friends) to minister to the poor in parishes where the prosperous had fled to the suburbs, to speak loathingly of social Darwinists (Neo-Cons, the FBI, the CIA, humorless, anal-retentive Republicans, and so on).

I myself was not changed by the war, except that I became entitled to converse as a peer with other combat veterans of any army, of any war. (To do so, in fact, gives me a fleeting taste of membership in Robert Redfield's Folk Society.) During the question-and-answer period following my speech at the National Air and Space Museum, I was asked what being bombed strategically had done to my personality. I replied that the war had been a great adventure for me, which I wouldn't have missed for anything, and that the principal shapers of my personality were probably neighborhood dogs when I was growing up. (Some were nice, some were mean. Some looked nice but were mean. Some looked mean but were nice.) This is true.

My second wife is another Episcopalian, and like my first one thinks that I have no religion and am a spiritual cripple on that account. When Jill's and my daughter Lily was baptized by the

Bishop of New York in the biggest Gothic church in the world
(in a neighborhood so poor that the Bishop couldn't get cable
service for his TV), I did not attend. (There is a sound reason
for hating me right there, but I think the main reason is cigarettes. O'Hare was buried with a pack of cigarettes and a book
of matches in his pocket. I don't think Jill would do that for
me, but you never know. Never prejudge anyone.)

In order not to seem a spiritual quadriplegic to strangers trying
to get a fix on me, I sometimes say I am a Unitarian Universalist
(I breathe). So that denomination claims me as one of its own.
It honored me by having me deliver a lecture at a gathering in
Rochester, New York, in June 1986. I began (almost exactly as
I would begin at the graduation ceremonies at the University of
Rhode Island):

"There was a newspaper humorist named Kin Hubbard in
my hometown of Indianapolis, where my ancestors were Freethinkers and then Unitarians—or not much of anything as far
as religious labels go. Kin Hubbard attended a graduation ceremony out there in Indiana. He commented afterward on the
graduation address to the departing seniors. He said it might
be better to spread out the really important stuff over four years
instead of saving it all up until the very end.

"I do not expect to flabbergast you tonight with all the really
important stuff. I know you are already well educated both in
a bookish sense and in the famous American School of Hard
Knocks.

"I myself seem to be coming across really important stuff very
late in life. I am sixty-three, but it was only two months ago
that I found a quotation from the works of Friedrich Wilhelm
Nietzsche, a contemporary of Mark Twain, which explains and
justifies the spiritual condition of myself, my Indiana ancestors,
and my children, and of Mark Twain as well, I think. Nietzsche
said in effect, and in German of course, that only a person of
great faith could afford to be a skeptic.

"So what we have here in Rochester tonight is a congregation of people who have faith. You have it in an era when so many Americans find the human condition meaningless that they are surrendering their will and their common sense to quacks and racketeers and charismatic lunatics. Bad preachers will give them faith for money, or in exchange for what little political power the frightened souls without faith may have in this pluralistic democracy.

"I listen to the ethical pronouncements of the leaders of the so-called religious revival going on in this country, including those of our President, and am able to distill only two firm commandments from them. The first commandment is this: 'Stop thinking.' The second commandment is this: 'Obey.' Only a person who has given up on the power of reason to improve life here on Earth, or a soldier in Basic Training could accept either commandment gladly: 'Stop thinking' and 'Obey.'

"I was an Infantry Private during World War II and fought against the Germans in Europe. My religion as well as my blood type was stamped into my dogtags. The Army decided my religion was P, for 'Protestant.' There is no room on dogtags for footnotes and a bibliography. In retrospect, I think they should have put S on my dogtags, for 'Saracen,' since we were fighting Christians who were on some sort of utterly insane Crusade. They had crosses on their flags and uniforms and all over their killing machines, just like the soldiers of the first Christian Emperor Constantine. And they lost, of course, which has to be acknowledged as quite a setback for Christianity.

"Now what is it, do you think, that makes Christians so bloodthirsty?

"I will tell you what my theory is, and I will be glad to hear yours after I am through standing up here and going 'Blah blah blah.' I think the problem is linguistic, and might be repaired, if the evangelists would only allow it, with startling simplicity. The Christian preachers exhort their listeners to love one another and to love their neighbors and so on. Love is simply too

strong a word to be of much use in ordinary, day-to-day rela-
tionships. Love is for Romeo and Juliet.

"I'm to love my neighbor? How can I do that when I'm not
even speaking to my wife and kids today? My wife said to me
the other day, after a knock-down-drag-out fight about interior
decoration, 'I don't love you anymore.' And I said to her, 'So
what else is new?' She really didn't love me then, which was
perfectly normal. She will love me some other time—I think, I
hope. It's possible.

"If she had wanted to terminate the marriage, to carry it past
the point of no return, she would have had to say, 'I don't
respect you anymore.' Now—that would be terminal.

"One of the many unnecessary American catastrophes going
on right now, along with the religious revival and plutonium,
is all the people who are getting divorced because they don't
love each other anymore. That is like trading in a car when the
ashtrays are full. When you don't *respect* your mate anymore—
that's when the transmission is shot and there's a crack in the
engine block.

"I like to think that Jesus said in Aramaic, 'Ye shall *respect*
one another.' That would be a sign to me that He really wanted
to help us here on Earth, and not just in the Afterlife. Then
again, He had no way of knowing what ludicrously high stan-
dards Hollywood was going to set for love. How many people
resemble Paul Newman or Meryl Streep?

"And look at the spectrum of emotions we think of auto-
matically when we hear the word 'love.' If you can't love your
neighbor, then you can at least like him. If you can't like him,
you can at least not give a damn about him. If you can't ignore
him, then you have to hate him, right? You've exhausted all the
other possibilities. That's a quick trip to hate, isn't it? And it
starts with love. It is such a logical trip, like the one from 'white-
hot' to 'ice-cold,' with 'red-hot,' 'hot,' 'warm,' 'tepid,' 'room
temperature,' 'cool,' 'chilly,' and 'freezing' in between. The spec-

trum of emotions suggested by the word 'love' again: 'love,' and then 'like,' and then 'don't give a damn about,' and then 'hate.'

"That is my explanation of why hatred is so common in that part of the world dominated by Christianity. There are all these people who have been told to do their best at loving. They fail, most of them. And why wouldn't they fail, since loving is extremely difficult? Most of these people are also failures as pole-vaulters and performers on the flying trapeze. And when they fail to love, day after day, year in and year out, come one, come all, the logic of the language leads them to the seemingly inevitable conclusion that they must hate instead. The step beyond hating, of course, is killing in imaginary self-defense.

" 'Ye shall respect one another.' Now there is something almost anybody in reasonable mental health can do day after day, year in and year out, come one, come all, to everyone's clear benefit. 'Respect' does not imply a spectrum of alternatives, some of them very dangerous. Respect is like a light switch. It is either on or off. And if we are no longer able to respect someone, we don't feel like killing that person. Our response is restrained. We simply want to make him or her feel like something the cat drug in.

"Compare making somebody feel like something the cat drug in with Armageddon or World War III.

"So there you have my scheme for making Christianity, which has killed so many people so horribly, a little less homicidal: substituting the word 'respect' for the word 'love.' And as I said, I have been in actual battle with people who had crosses all over themselves. They were sure no fun.

"I have little hope that my simple reform will attract any appreciable support during my lifetime, anyway, or in the lifetimes of my children. The Christian quick trip from love to hate and murder is our principal entertainment. We might call it 'Christianity Fails Again,' and how satisfying so many of us have been trained to find it when it fails and fails.

"In America it takes the form of the cowboy story. A good-hearted, innocent young man rides into town, with friendly intentions toward one and all. Never mind that he happens to be wearing a loaded Colt .44 on either hip. The last thing he wants is trouble. But before he knows it, this loving man is face to face with another man, who is so unlovable that he has absolutely no choice but to shoot him. Christianity Fails Again.

"Very early British versions are tales of the quests of the Christian knights of King Arthur's Camelot. Like Hermann Göring, they have crosses all over them. They ride out into the countryside to help the weak, an admirably Christian activity. They are certainly not looking for trouble. Never mind that they are iron Christmas trees decorated with the latest in weaponry. And before they know it, they are face to face with other knights so unlovable that they have absolutely no choice but to chop them up as though they were sides of beef in a butcher shop. Christianity Fails Again. What fun! And I point out to you that there was an implied promise that our own government would entertain us with failures of Christianity when John F. Kennedy allowed his brief Presidency to be called Camelot.

"And how does our present federal administration, which has become just one more big corporation fighting for our attention on television and in the newspapers, propose to maintain its popularity? With the same old tried and true story, which begins with friendly, open people, who say such things as 'Nobody wants peace more than we do' and 'Nobody is slower to anger than we are' and so on. And then, all of a sudden, 'Ka-boom, ka-boom!' Christianity Fails Again.

"The place where it failed most recently, incidentally, which is Libya, has a population less than that of greater Chicago, Illinois. And should any Christian be sorry that we killed Qaddafi's baby daughter? Well—Jerry Falwell should speak to this issue, since he knows all the verses in the Bible which make murder acceptable. My own theory is that the little girl, by allowing herself to be adopted by a dark-skinned Muslim absolutely nobody watching American television could love, in effect committed suicide.

"Perhaps the CIA could find out if she had been despondent before cashing in.

"But I digress.

"I have come all the way to Rochester to speak to a congregation of persons of such deep faith that they dare to be skeptical about widely accepted pronouncements of what life is all about, who call themselves Unitarian Universalists. So I should surely offer an opinion as to the present condition of that relatively small denomination.

"I will say that you, in terms of numbers, power, and influence, and your spiritual differences with the general population, are analogous to the earliest Christians in the catacombs under Imperial Rome. I hasten to add that your hardships are not the same, nor are you in any danger. Nobody in the power structure thinks children of the Age of Reason amount to a hill of beans. That is the extent of your discomfort. That sure beats being crucified upside down or being fed to the carnivorous menagerie at the Circus Maximus.

"You are like the early Christians in yearning for an era of peace and plenty and justice, which may never come. They thought Jesus would bring that about. You think human beings should be able to create such an era through their own efforts.

"You are like them, as I have already said, in that you live in a time when killing is a leading entertainment form. According to the American Academy of Pediatrics, the average American child watches 18,000 TV murders before it graduates from high school. That kid has seen Christianity fail with pistols and rifles and shotguns and machine guns. It has seen Christianity fail with guillotines and gallows and electric chairs and gas chambers. That youngster has seen Christianity fail with fighter planes and bombers and tanks and battleships and submarines—with hatchets and clubs and chain saws and butcher knives. And afterward that boy or girl is supposed to feel grateful to the corporations, our Federal Government among them, which put on such shows.

"Romans as rich and powerful as modern corporations used to put on such shows, so we can say that all that has changed is the sponsorship.

"Like the early Christians, you are part of a society dominated by superstitions, by pure baloney. During Roman Imperial times, though, pure baloney was all that was available about the size of the planet, about its place in the cosmos, about the natures of its other inhabitants, about the probable origins of life, about the causes and cures of diseases, about chemistry, about physics, about biology, and on and on. Everybody, including the early Christians, had no choice but to be full of baloney. That is not the case today. And my goodness, do we ever have a lot of information now, and proven techniques for creating almost anything in abundance and for moderating all sorts of catastrophes.

"How tragic it is, then, that the major impulses in this and several other societies nowadays should be in the direction of the pure baloney and cruel entertainments of thousands of years ago, which almost inevitably lead to the antithesis of beauty and the good life and Christianity as taught by Jesus Christ, which is war.

"When I say that the Unitarian Universalists, the people who know pure baloney when they hear it, are something like the early Christians in the catacombs, am I suggesting that contempt for baloney will someday be as widespread as Christianity is today? Well—the example of Christianity is not encouraging, actually, since it was nothing but a poor people's religion, a servant's religion, a slave's religion, a woman's religion, a child's religion, and would have remained such if it hadn't stopped taking the Sermon on the Mount seriously and joined forces with the vain and rich and violent. I can't imagine that you would want to do that, to give up everything you believe in order to play a bigger part in world history.

"You would need a logo—something you could put on T-shirts and flags to start with, and then maybe on the sides of tanks and airplanes and peacekeeping missiles later on. If you really want a logo, I recommend a circle with a baloney sausage in the middle, and with a bar across the sausage—meaning, in international sign language, 'No baloney.'

"But then, in order to recruit a large and enthusiastic following, perhaps even a rabid following, you would have to repudiate that symbol—without saying so, of course. You would have to make up a lot of highly emotional baloney, which you surely don't have now—all about what God wants and doesn't want, whom He likes, whom He hates, what He eats for breakfast. The more complete picture of God you can cobble together, the better you'll do.

"The more violent picture of Him you create, the better you'll do. I say this as an expert, as a former advertising and publicity man. The President and I came out of the same division at General Electric. And there he is in the White House, and here I am speaking to some obscure religious sect in Rochester. But that's another story. My point is that if you are going to succeed as a mass movement, you are going to do it on television and videocassettes or nowhere, and any God you invent is going to be up against *Miami Vice* and Clint Eastwood and Sylvester Stallone. Stallone, incidentally, was a girls' gym teacher in Switzerland during the Vietnam War. You look into those spaniel eyes of his, and you know just how hard he tried to love before he started killing socialist wogs and gooks.

"And stay clear of the Ten Commandments, as do the television evangelists. Those things are booby-trapped, because right in the middle of them is one commandment which would, if taken seriously, cripple modern religion as show business. It is this commandment: 'Thou shalt not kill.'

"I thank you for your attention." (The end.)

I was preaching to the choir, so to speak. In more conventionally religious venues, my Freethinking has proved less digestible. So that after I spoke at Transylvania University in Lexington, Kentucky, in October 1990, the Dean of the Chapel there, the Reverend Paul H. Jones, wrote a troubled letter to a mutual friend, from which I have his permission to quote in part. "Why am I so depressed as I read *Hocus Pocus*?" he asked. "Don't I like the human condition as he portrays it via the characters, situations, educational system? The world is disintegrating. Does that accurately reflect life? Where am I in that world? With whom do I identify? Why don't I like it?"

He goes on: "I want to ask Vonnegut about his religious persuasion. What is redemptive about his writings? Must they be? Are they intended to be? Am I imposing or asking too much? He deliberately mentioned Jesus and invoked religious images. What gives?"

My reply is the next-to-last thing in the Appendix.

(As for my pacifism, it is nothing if not ambivalent. When I ask myself what person in American history I would most like to have been, I am powerless to protest when my subconscious nominates Joshua L. Chamberlain. Colonel Chamberlain, while in command of the 20th Maine Volunteers during the Civil War, ordered a downhill and then uphill bayonet charge which turned the tide of battle in favor of the Union forces at Gettysburg.)

© Hope Rosenberg; courtesy of the photographer and CARE

XVII

" 'Who are the good guys and who are the bad guys in Mozambique?' I asked.

"I was strapped into the seat of a jet bound from Johannesburg, South Africa, to Maputo, the capital of the former Portuguese colony of Mozambique, on the east coast of Africa, where I had never been before. All I knew about it so far was that it was as beautiful and habitable as California, had several good ports on one of the longest shorelines of any African nation, was underpopulated, got enough rain most years and sounded like a Garden of Eden—but was a manmade hell instead."

Thus began a piece I wrote for *Parade* at the start of 1990, when the so-called Communist Bloc of nations could no longer hold up their end of the Harry High School myth that there was a desperate struggle between good and evil societies going on. (When I was a student at Shortridge High School, whose colors were blue and white, we hated Arsenal Tech, whose colors were green and white. One time I got roughed up by a bunch of Tech subhumans while I was walking home alone from a Shortridge–Tech football game wearing a Shortridge band uniform. As I would tell Benny Goodman many years later, "I used to play a little licorice-stick myself.")

"The stranger I asked about the good guys and the bad guys was a white American male named John Yale, who was an old hand in Mozambique," my *Parade* piece went on. "He was a worker for World Vision, an American evangelical Christian charity, which was getting food and clothing and other bare essentials to some of the country's more than 1 million helpless refugees. The population of the whole country was only 15 million—fewer people than are crowded into Mexico City nowadays. The refugees had been driven off their little farms and had had their homes and schools and hospitals burned down by other Mozambicans who called themselves in Portuguese the National Resistance of Mozambique, or RENAMO for short."

(Our Neo-Conservatives, or Neo-Cons for short, think RENAMO is the cat's pajamas. I heard from several of them after the piece was published, and their letters reminded me of the way Dean Martin introduced Frank Sinatra once. He said Sinatra was going to tell about all of the *good* things the Mafia was doing.)

"John Yale replied that his job was not to choose sides in a civil war but to help people in deep trouble—no matter who or what they were said to be. But I sensed from some of the other carefully neutral things he said about RENAMO, which had been raping and murdering and pillaging and all that since 1976, when it was trained and equipped by white South Africans and Rhodesians, that it shouldn't be thought of as people. RENAMO had become an incurable disease instead, out of control, since the armed forces were so poor and spread so thin, a ghastly feature of daily life no more to be discussed in terms of good and evil than cholera, say, or bubonic plague.

"There is, in fact, an old, old word in every language for roving gangs of heartless hit-and-run robbers, gangs which have become a crippling or fatal disease, unreasoning, existing for their own sake and nothing more. In English the word is *bandits*. In Portuguese it is *bandidos,* which, I would soon learn, in Maputo and elsewhere was a synonym for RENAMO.

" 'Crippling or fatal disease' did I say? Our own State Department estimates that RENAMO, virtually unopposed, has killed more than 100,000 Mozambicans since 1987 alone—including at least 8,000 children under the age of five, most of whom were driven into the bush, where they starved to death. Our own government may have supported RENAMO secretly in the past, because Mozambique was avowedly Marxist, and South Africa used to do so openly and unashamedly. But no more. The *bandidos* are so few, and so hated, for good reason, that they can never expect to take over the country. Everybody else—including the United States and the Soviet Union and the International Red Cross and CARE and John Yale of World Vision—is doing everything possible to ease the agony of the non-Marxist, noncapitalist, nearly naked, and utterly pitiful refugees. For that matter, by the time I got there, the few Mozambicans sophisticated enough to have some idea of how Marxism was supposed to work were as sick of Socialist idealism in practice as anybody in Moscow or Warsaw or East Berlin.

"I was soon off the jet and into an eight-seat twin-engine Cessna flown by a lantern-jawed kid named Jim Friesen, who had previously been a bush pilot in northwest Canada. Jim couldn't fly low to give us a closer look at the sights because the *bandidos* could be anywhere in the open country. They shot at boats and planes and trucks and cars, at anything that looked as if it might have something to do with making the lives of the common people less hellish. Our chartered Cessna wasn't a luxury. It was a necessity, since all the roads below us had been turned into death traps by *bandido* ambushes and mines."

(Before I left, somebody asked me if I wasn't afraid of getting killed, and I said, "I'm just going to Mozambique, not the South Bronx.")

"Imagine California with all its roads cut, with most of its country people driven into towns and cities, with its farms abandoned, and with its huddled, defenseless population having to be fed and clothed by air. Welcome to Mozambique.

"From October 9 to October 13, while Wall Street was having a little crash, Jim Friesen flew me and several others with media contacts in the USA—including reporters from *The New York Times* and *The Washington Post* and *Newsweek* and CNN— from one isolated and besieged refugee center to another. What we saw wasn't all that different from what every adult American has seen more than enough of in photographs, whether they were taken in liberated Nazi death camps or Biafra or the Sudan or you name it. I myself have seen people that hungry in real life—at the end of World War II in Germany, where I was a PW, and again on the Biafran side of the Nigerian civil war."

(In my novel *Bluebeard* I describe a valley full of refugees at the end of WW II. It wasn't imaginary. It was real. O'Hare and I were there.)

"In Mozambique we saw lots of familiar stuff, stupefied starving children with eyes as big as dinner plates, adults with chests that looked like bird cages. There was one new sight for me anyway: purposely mutilated people with their noses or ears or whatever cut off by hand-held sharp instruments."

(I didn't just hear about them. I saw them and talked to them through an interpreter. They weren't brought to us. They were just faces, what was left of them, in a great big crowd of people who could easily be dead soon for want of calories.)

"We were making this gruesome trip at the invitation of CARE, a bigger and older relief organization than John Yale's. CARE hoped that we would let ordinary Americans know about the peculiarly manmade agony of faraway Mozambique, and what so many relief agencies to which they might have contributed were doing there."

(CARE came into being after World War II, of course, bringing food to people starving in the ruins of Europe. It had since ministered to Third World people in dire need, but an executive in its New York City headquarters told me that, what with the collapse of the Russian Empire, CARE might have to return to certain parts of Europe again, mainly with storage batteries and tractor tires and so on. The chief piece of farm machinery in Mozambique was one of the world's worst polluters, since the farmers there cleared fields by burning them. RENAMO should be thanked, maybe, for making so many of them stop doing that.)

"With us was CARE's boss in Mozambique, David P. Neff, forty-three years old, whose hometown, which he hadn't seen in quite some time, was New Athens, Illinois. He had been in the Peace Corps in Cameroon, instead, and had then been hired by CARE, mastering shipping and accounting and hard-edge management techniques for getting relief supplies to where they were most needed—on time, unspoiled, and unstolen—to the people the donors had addressed them to, in Liberia and then in the Gaza Strip and then in the Philippines and then in Somalia and then in Sierra Leone. And now Mozambique. His enemy wasn't RENAMO. It was inefficiency."

(Will Dave and his family next take up residence and learn the language and the customs in Warsaw or Leningrad?)

"I won't repeat the tales of hunger Dave had to tell. As I say, color the people in old photographs of Auschwitz all shades of brown and black and you will be looking at what he sees every day. I will pass on instead what he said to me as we were flying over a refugee center near the mouth of the crocodile-infested Zambezi River, at a town called Marromeu. We flew over the town before landing, making sure that the people were out in the open, trying to scratch a living with their hoes from their little gardens, and not hiding in the bush from yet another hit-and-run attack by what some Americans still call 'Freedom Fighters.' Dave said that keeping RENAMO in mines and bullets and rocket launchers was so cheap that they didn't need South Africa or the CIA or whatever to support them. He estimated the price at about $4 million a year, the cost of a movie without big stars or of a fairly elaborate Broadway musical. This was a sum from a few rich individuals outside Mozambique, or even one billionaire.

"Dave added that if the *bandidos* actually captured the capital city of Maputo, which they could probably do, since they were operating on its outskirts, they would look around helplessly and ask in effect, 'Okay, what are we supposed to do now?' All they knew about transportation was how to shoot at anything that dared to move. All they knew about hospitals and schools was how to burn them down or blow them up.

"The hungry and terrified and dispossessed farmers in and around Marromeu were out in the open. They had surely never heard of Karl Marx, and probably had never even heard of Johannesburg or New York or Moscow. So Jim brought our plane down expertly on the short, rough landing strip. To one side was the corpse of a DC-3 which had cracked up a couple of days before. Fifteen minutes earlier we had been looking down at about a hundred wild elephants.

"Dave and Jim knew the plane well. Its nickname was 'Little Annie.' She had been delivering supplies to refugees day after day for years. But now her landing gear had given out, and her belly was all ripped to hell. She had to have been older than Dave Neff. The last DC-3 was built in 1946, when CARE was sending food parcels to the ruins of Europe and the black people of Mozambique had thirty more years of virtual slavery to endure under the rule of the Portuguese.

"Among the first Mozambicans we saw after landing were two gaunt men wearing shirts Little Annie must have brought them. One shirt was decorated with the flags of United States yacht clubs. The other was emblazoned with an S in a triangle, which identified the wearer as the man who was mild-mannered Clark Kent in private life—but who now stood before us as Superman."

(That ends my piece for *Parade*. I wrote another for the Op-

Ed page of *The New York Times,* but I can't find it now, and the hell with it anyway. In it, I remember, I pointed out that the black people of Mozambique threw out their Portuguese masters, who hadn't even allowed them to drive motor vehicles, when we were about to be thrown out of Vietnam. That was how young they were as a nation. And one of the first things they wanted to do was learn how to read and write and do a little math. RENAMO is still doing its best to keep them from doing that—with state-of-the-art weapons and communications equipment which are still coming from God knows where. When the Portuguese were departing so long ago now, they poured cement down the sewer lines of toilets in office buildings and hotels and hospitals and so on which weren't going to belong to them anymore.)

In my book *Palm Sunday* I reprinted an essay I wrote when I came home from the Biafran side of the Nigerian civil war. The Biafrans (rebel Ibos) were so successfully blockaded that their children all had red hair and their rectums were everted, dangling outside like radiator hoses and so on, thanks to protein deficiency. When I got back to my own country (where my family was off skiing in Vermont), I got a room at the old Royalton Hotel in Manhattan, and I found myself crying so hard I was barking like a dog. I didn't come close to doing that after World War II. Nor did I shed one tear after getting back from Mozambique. The last time I cried (and I did it quietly, and didn't bark like a dog) was when my first wife Jane (who was skiing when I was in Biafra) died. (Our son the doctor, Mark, said after her death that he himself would not have submitted to the ghastly treatments which allowed Jane to stay alive with cancer for so long.)

I ran into an old friend from Shortridge High School, a great inventor and mechanical engineer named Herb Harrington, while I was writing my dry-eyed piece about Mozambique. I confessed that something had happened to me since Biafra, that Mozambique had impressed me intellectually but not emotionally. I told Herb that I had seen little girls about the age of my own precious Lily drifting off to death, having been in the bush too long before reaching a refugee center, but that I felt hardly anything afterward. He said that the same thing had happened to him when he was in the Army during World War II, with a small crew installing radio stations along the coast of China. Wagonloads of Chinese who had starved to death were a common sight, and he soon (in less than a week) no longer noticed them.

(The photograph at the head of this chapter shows me in action in Mozambique, demonstrating muscular Christianity in an outfit that might have been designed by Ralph Lauren. The aborigines didn't know whether to shit or go blind until I showed up. And then I fixed everything.)

XVIII

Ed Wynn's joke about the woman whose house was on fire (and who had put water on it, to no avail) is the funniest *clean* joke in the world. The funniest dirty joke in the world was told to me by my translator in Moscow, Rita Rait, who died in her late eighties a few years ago. (She was a language genius, a Robert Burns scholar, the translator of me and J. D. Salinger and Sinclair Lewis and John Steinbeck from English, of Franz Kafka from German, and on and on. Jill and I spent some time with her in Paris, where she was doing research in documents all in French.) During World War II she was an interpreter for American and British freighter crews bringing food and ammunition to Murmansk in northwest Russia (on the icy Barents Sea) while under constant attack by German planes and submarines. She could replicate several British accents flawlessly and told us this story in cockney.

The bare bones of the world's funniest dirty story (without Rita to do the cockney) are as follows: An eccentric British millionaire died and left what was to be an enormous prize for the wittiest original limerick. He acknowledged in his will that the wittiest limericks tended to be the bawdiest as well, so that ribaldry (even of the coarsest sort) was not to disqualify any entry for the prize. So a blue-ribbon (but not bluenose) jury was formed and limericks arrived by the ton. People (being British) could talk of nothing else. The jurors at last announced that the contest had been won by a housewife in East Anglia. Their decision was not only unanimous but hilarious. The winning entry was surely the wittiest limerick in the world, but unfortunately so obscene that it could never be made public in any form.

The country of course went mad with curiosity, as would anybody upon hearing the premise of this perfect tale. The judges were adamant in both their delight with the winning limerick and their belief that the civilized world could never weather its indecency. So everybody went after the author, a suddenly rich and famous housewife, the seeming soul of propriety. (When telling this story, which she had heard from a British sailor, Rita became that housewife, simultaneously priggish and smug about the bottomless reserve of filthy thoughts which had enabled her to win the contest.) She agreed with the judges that her prize entry was so offensive, although brilliantly witty, that there was no alternative to their and her carrying the five lines to their graves. Winston Churchill himself, however, since the war effort had come to a halt because of her, prevailed on her to go on the BBC and recite her limerick, using the empty sound "dah" for the syllable of any word unfit for the ears of a family audience.

So she did it.

This was the bowdlerized limerick which went out over the air:

> *Dah dah dah dah dah dah* dah *dah,*
> *Dah dah dah dah dah dah dah* dah *dah!*
> *Dah* dah dah dah *dah,*

Dah dah dah dah *dah!*
Dah dah dah dah *fucking cunt.*

Rita (who was a Russian native but had a Scottish ancestor, hence her un-Russian last name) told us that story, and then she chirped with all possible cuteness, "English is not my language, so I can say whatever I please in it, no matter how dirty. What freedom! What fun!"

Translators should be paid the same royalties as authors. I have said so to several of my foreign publishers, offering to take less for myself in order that the translator might get more. I might just as well have told them that the world was flat and I could prove it. In November 1983, I spoke as follows to a gathering of translators at Columbia University:

"The first nation to publish me in a language other than English was West Germany, which brought out my first novel, *Player Piano* (Scribner's, 1952), under the title *Das Höllische System* in 1964. The translator, Wulf H. Bergner, was so familiar with American English that he felt no need to ask me what I had meant by this or that. I do not mock him by saying so. This was truly the case. I am told that his is a fine translation. I take other people's word for this, although I have some rudimentary familiarity with German. For reasons I am not prepared to explain, I can't stand to read myself even in English. To give a name to this primitive neurosis: let us call it perpetual embarrassment.

"I had a lot more fun with the book's next translator, Roberta Rambelli of Genoa, Italy. She sent me the first letter I ever got from a translator. I still remember two of her delightful questions: 'What is a rumble seat? What is a Ferris wheel?' I was pleased to tell her what few Americans know: The Ferris wheel was invented as a device to elevate artillery spotters above the treetops for the Grand Army of the Republic during our Civil War.

"It would be seven years before I would write another novel.

This was not because of spiritual difficulties. This was because of financial difficulties. It costs a lot of money for a writer to support a family while he or she writes a book. For seven years I did not have the money.

"The second book was *The Sirens of Titan* (Dell, 1959), and the French were the first foreigners to pick it up. Their translator, Monique Theis, had no questions to put to me. I am told that many of her misunderstandings of American English are ludicrous. But then my old friend Roberta Rambelli wrote to say that she had again been hired to explain me to Italians, and she had about fifty-three questions for me—what was this, what was that? I was in love with her by then, and I dare to suggest that she was in love with me.

"Soon after that, my son Mark, who would himself become not only a writer but a pediatrician, went to Europe with money he had earned as a shellfisherman on Cape Cod. I urged him to visit my friend Roberta in Genoa, which he did. I myself had never met Roberta or seen Italy. He presented himself at her dwelling there, and she was clearly thrilled to see him. But they had to converse on paper, as though both of them were deaf and dumb. She could not understand spoken English, she could only read and write that language—my situation in French, by the way. Is this an ironical story? I say this: Not in the least. It is beautiful.

"Both books were pirated by the Soviet Union, which back then would have nothing to do with the capitalist plot known as the International Copyright Convention. I heard nothing from my translators there, which was nothing new, since, as I have said, I was given the same silent treatment by my translators in Germany, and France, and then in Denmark and Holland, as well.

"I am sixty-one years old now, and there have been a lot of books and translators since then. I used to make fun of my French translators, since people told me they did preposterous jobs, and I never heard from them, and people never seemed to like me much when I went to France. But the French translator of my last two books, Robert Pépin, also a novelist, speaks American English better than I do, and has become a close friend of mine. Not only that, but as fluent in American English as he is, his letters to me ask more good questions, even, than did those of dear Roberta Rambelli, who is in Heaven now.

"And while I continue to express annoyance that the Soviet Union pays me nothing when publishing works of mine which were written before it joined the Copyright Convention and pays me next to nothing for what I have written since, I have become fonder of my translator over there, Rita Rait, than I am of anybody else outside my own family. We first met in Paris, by arrangement, and then I went to visit her twice in Moscow and once in Leningrad. Even if she weren't my translator, I think we would be crazy about each other as human beings.

"There are some obscenities in my books, since I make Americans, and particularly soldiers, speak as they really speak. The modern Russian equivalents of these words cannot be set in type in the USSR. Before translating me, Rita Rait had confronted the same problem with J. D. Salinger's *Catcher in the Rye*. What did she do? It seems that there is an archaic peasant vocabulary for discussing barnyard matters which is regarded as inoffensive folklore, although it deals directly with excrement and sexual intercourse and so on. She used those words rather than modern obscenities when translating Salinger and me. Thus were we fairly represented.

"I could ramble on and on. The trouble I caused translators by naming a book *Jailbird* is worth an essay by itself. It turns out that countries older than my own have no word for persons who find themselves locked up again and again, since the penitentiary system, an invention of American Quakers, is so new. The closest European languages could come was with their words 'gallows bird.' This failed to describe the habitual criminal I had written about, since a person cannot be hanged again and again.

"Finally, every translator has had to totally rename the book.

"*Und so weiter.* If I have taken this opportunity to recall translators who have been particularly friendly, it is not to argue that sociability is an essential part of the process. All I require of a translator is that he or she be a more gifted writer than I am, and in at least two languages, one of them mine.

"And now I must get back to answering my mail, and especially a chatty letter from my Japanese translator, Mr. Shigeo Tobita, who wants to know, among other things, referring to something I have written, 'What is "Four Roses"? An expensive bottle of wine?'

"No. Four Roses is not quite the same thing as wine." (End of speech.)

Five months after saying that to the translators (not that there was any connection), I was carted off to the Emergency Room of St. Vincent's Hospital in the middle of the night to be pumped out. I had tried to kill myself. It wasn't a cry for help. It wasn't a nervous breakdown. I wanted "The Big Sleep" (Raymond Chandler). I wanted to "Slam the Big Door" (John D. Mac-Donald). No more jokes and no more coffee and no more cigarettes:

I wanted *out* of here.

(Near the end of the Appendix you can find an essay I wrote long afterward about possible connections between creativity and mental illness.)

XIX

The great fiction writer Ray Bradbury (who can't drive an automobile) made up a story called "The Kilimanjaro Device," which was about a person who could somehow undo ignominious suicides (or maybe ignominious anythings). He had a kind of magic Jeep, and he was driving it along a wilderness road near Ketchum, Idaho. He saw this terminally depressed, grizzled old bearded man, potbellied, trudging all alone. This was Ernest Hemingway, who would soon blow off his head with a shotgun. Bradbury's person in the magic Jeep offered him a lift to a better death than the one he was headed for. If Hemingway got in, he would die in an airplane crash on the peak of Mount Kilimanjaro (19,340 feet) in Tanzania, Africa. So Hemingway got in and died glamorously.

(The French writer Louis-Ferdinand Céline wrote about a doctor friend who was obsessed with expiring with dignity and who died in convulsions under a grand piano.)

It is possible in Ray Bradbury country that my own suicide was as successful as Hemingway's, that I am dead, that all I am seeing now is what might have been, if only I hadn't ended it all. This could be a lesson. As the man said when they strapped him into the electric chair in Cook County Jail years ago, "This will certainly teach me a lesson."

If all this is only what might have been (and I am moldering in my grave like my childhood idol, the bank robber John Dillinger), then I have to exclaim, "My goodness, I would have written at least four more books!" and so on. If only I had lived, I would have heard my daughter Lily singing a song she learned at summer camp:

> *Boys go to Jupiter to get stupider!*
> *Girls go to college to get more knowledge!*
> *Boys go to Venus to get another penis!*
> *Girls drink Pepsi so they can be sexy!*

If I hadn't been too pissed off to live another minute (absolutely apeshit), I would have published this swell essay in *The New York Times* in the spring of 1990:

"For whatever reason, American humorists or satirists or whatever you want to call them, those who choose to laugh rather than weep about demoralizing information, become intolerably unfunny pessimists if they live past a certain age. If Lloyd's of London offered policies promising to compensate comical writers for loss of sense of humor, its actuaries could count on such a loss occurring, on average, at age sixty-three for men, and for women at twenty-nine, say.

"My generalization is happily or unhappily confirmed in a book called *Punchlines* (Paragon House, 1990) by William Keough of the English Department of Fitchburg State College in Massachusetts. The subtitle is *The Violence of American Humor*. Mr. Keough, by means of essays on Mark Twain, Ring Lardner, Ambrose Bierce, myself, comedians in the movies (both silents and talkies), and radio and TV and nightclub comics right up to the present, persuades me that the most memorable jokes by Americans are responses to the economic and physical violence of this society. 'How often does it seem that the American humorist, having set out daringly and lightly as an amused observer of the American spectacle of violence and corruption, ends up mouthing sardonic fables in a bed of gloom,' he writes.

"So guess what: My latest novel, *Hocus Pocus,* to be published in September, is a sardonic fable in a bed of gloom.

"Inevitable.

" 'Violence, the inspiration of much American humor, outlives it,' says Mr. Keough. 'When the jokes grow cold, the guns—unfortunately—are still hot.'

"Mark Twain finally stopped laughing at his own agony and that of those around him. He denounced life on this planet as a crock. He died. He hadn't lived long enough to hear about nuclear weapons. He was dead as a doornail before he could even hear about World War I.

"Jokes work this way: The jokester frightens the listener just a little bit, by mentioning something challenging, such as sex or physical danger, or suggesting that the listener is having his or her intelligence tested. Step two: The jokester makes clear that no intelligent response is required of the listener. This leaves the listener stuck with useless fight-or-flee chemicals in his or her bloodstream, which must be gotten rid of somehow, unless the listener wants to slug the jokester or do jumping jacks.

"What the listener most likely will do is expel those chemicals through the lungs with quick expansions and contractions of the chest cavity, accompanied by grotesque facial expressions and barking sounds.

"Intelligence test: 'Why did the chicken cross the road?' Sex: 'A traveling salesman's car broke down on a country road on a stormy night. He knocked on a farmer's door, and the farmer said, "You can spend the night, but you'll have to sleep with my daughter." ' Physical danger: 'A man fell off a cliff. Halfway down he grabbed a sapling. So there he was, hanging by his hands, with certain death a thousand feet below him.'

"But jokesters are all through when they find themselves talking about challenges so real and immediate and appalling to their listeners that no amount of laughter can make the listeners feel safe and perfectly well again. I found myself doing that on a speaking tour of campuses in the spring of 1989, and canceled all future engagements. That wasn't at all what I enjoyed doing to audiences, and yet there I was doing it. I wondered out loud onstage, for instance, what I and my brother and sister and our parents might have done if we had been German citizens when Hitler came to power. Any reply would be moot, but almost certainly depressing. And then I said that the whole world faced a problem far worse than the rise of another Hitler, which was our destruction of the planet as a life-supporting apparatus of delicate and beautiful complexity.

"I said that one day fairly soon we would all go belly-up like guppies in a neglected fishbowl. I suggested an epitaph for the whole planet, which was: 'We could have saved it, but we were too darn cheap and lazy.'

"It really was time to quit.

"My Lord, I think I even said—in fact I know I said—that humanity itself had become an unstoppable glacier made of hot meat, which ate up everything in sight and then made love, and then doubled in size again. I topped that off with a stage aside to the effect that the Pope in Rome was of no help when it came to slowing down the meat.

"Enough!

"It seemed possible to me, though, that I might still be amusing on paper, hooking people with little barbless hooks and then letting them off again. Writing a book, after all, is a slow and deliberate activity, like making flowered wallpaper for a ballroom by hand. Since I knew how jokes worked, hooking and releasing, I could still make them, even though I no longer felt like making them. I remembered that my father got sick of being an architect, when he was about ten years younger than I am, actually, but he went on doing architecture.

"As a good friend pointed out to me one time, my ideas have everything but originality. That was my fate. So I came up with the wholly unoriginal idea of writing a *Don Quixote* set in modern times. There might be a certain amount of freshness to my tale, I hoped, if I gave an affectionate razzing to what had long been my dream of an ideal citizen. Although Mr. Keough doesn't say so, I think all American humorists, when saying how flawed American citizens really are, would not be interested in doing that if they did not have clear images in their heads of what American citizens ought to be. Dreams of ideal citizens are as essential to our humorists, in my opinion, as they were to Karl Marx and Thomas Jefferson.

"But it didn't come out very funny. There wasn't any way to let readers off the hook, off the Montauk Umbrella of modern times.

"A Montauk Umbrella is a fishing rig favored by sports fishermen putting out to sea in motor yachts from the easternmost town on the South Fork of Long Island. It is like the spread ribs of an umbrella stripped of its cloth and handle. At the tip of each rib is a steel wire leader. At the end of each leader is a counterfeit squid made of off-white surgical tubing. Sticking out through a slit in each tube is a hook with a barb so big and sharp that any bluefish or bass that strikes at it or any other lure in the fast-moving galaxy of seeming tasty tidbits can never get off again.

"There is no contemporary equivalent to the unhooking device Mark Twain was able to use with success before World War I and World War II and all the rest of it, at the end of possibly the blackest of all well-known American comic novels, *Huckleberry Finn*. This, of course, was the unhooking: Huck, resourceful and tough and adorable, and with most of his life still ahead of him, says he is going to 'light out for the territory.'

"Rocky Flats, Colorado, maybe? Or how about Hanford, Washington, or the shores of Prince William Sound in Alaska? Or how about lighting out for Twain's own intended destination when he himself lit out from Hannibal—the virgin wilderness of the Amazon?" (The end.)

Not only would I have written that if I hadn't died, but I would have rejoiced in the birth of three more grandchildren. I already had three. My mother never saw any of her one dozen grandchildren, although my sister Alice was pregnant with her first one, Jim, when Alice and I found Mother dead. (No prospect of good news, obviously, could rescue Mother. She felt as awful as anybody does nowadays in Mozambique, where there is no end to murdering but almost no suicide.)

But to heck with the premise that all I am experiencing now is what might have been if I hadn't cashed in my chips in the Emergency Room of St. Vincent's Hospital six years ago. I am alive, still smoking and wearing my father's mournful mustache. (My brother wears it, too.) *Cogito ergo sum.*

I have actually written an essay in praise of something, of the reading of books, for a 1990 Christmas catalogue sent to the best customers of the Kroch's & Brentano's bookstores in Chicago. It goes like this:

"I was willing to believe back in the 1960s that deep meditation as practiced in India might be a way to achieve happiness and wisdom which had not been previously available to people of European and African stock. The Beatles also believed this for a while. I doubt that the late, great (I mean it) Abbie Hoffman ever believed it. He wasn't about to give up his frenzied sense of humor, the sanest thing in this country during the Vietnam War, in exchange for personal, inner peace.

"I would have been glad to make that swap. I delivered myself to Maharishi Mahesh Yogi, as had the Beatles, to learn how to do Transcendental Meditation, or TM. I did not know the Beatles, and never heard their ultimate opinion of TM. I seem to recall that they broke up with the Maharishi over matters having nothing to do with Eastern-style semi-trances. My own impression was that TM was a nice little nap, but that not much happened, whether for good or ill. It was like scuba diving in lukewarm bouillon. A pink silk scarf might drift slowly by. That was big news down there.

"You awoke unchanged from a pleasant state between sleep and wakefulness.

"But I got more from my TM experiment than naps. When I sat upright in a straight chair, as the Maharishi had told me, and ignored niggling distractions and repeated my mantra ('aye-eem') externally and then internally, I realized that I had done the same sort of thing thousands of times before.

"I had done it while reading books!

"Since I was eight or so, I had been internalizing the written words of persons who had seen and felt things new to me instead of 'aye-eem, aye-eem, aye-eem.' The world dropped away when I did it. When I read an absorbing book, my pulse and respiration rate slowed down perceptibly, just as though I were doing TM.

"I was *already* a veteran meditator. When I awoke from my Western-style meditation I was often a wiser human being. And I tell this story because so many people nowadays regard printed pages as nothing more than obsolescent technology, first developed by the Chinese two thousand years ago. Books came into being, surely, as practical schemes for transmitting or storing information, no more romantic in Gutenberg's time than a computer in ours. It so happens, though—a wholly unforeseen accident—that the feel and appearance of a book when combined with a literate person in a straight chair can create a spiritual condition of priceless depth and meaning.

"This form of meditation, an accident, as I say, may be the greatest treasure at the core of our civilization. So we should never give up books, surrendering only crass and earthly matters to the printout and the cathode tube." (The end.)

(Xanthippe, with a career and income all her own, continues to empty chamber pots on my head from time to time. If it weren't for her I think I probably would have died of too much sleep long ago. I would have napped myself to death. At the very least I would have stopped seeing movies and plays, and reading books and magazines, and going outside, things like that. She is what George Bernard Shaw called "a life force woman.")

I mentioned Abbie Hoffman in that piece about books as mantras for meditation. I realize that most people nowadays don't know who he was or what he did. He was a clowning genius, having come into the world that way, like Lenny Bruce and Jack Benny and Ed Wynn and Stan Laurel and W. C. Fields and the Marx Brothers and Red Skelton and Fred Allen and Woody Allen and so on. He was a member of my children's generation. He is high on my list of saints, of exceptionally courageous, unarmed, unsponsored, unpaid souls who have tried to slow down even a little bit state crimes against those Jesus Christ said should inherit the Earth someday.

He did this with truth, anger, and ridicule.

He spent the last years of his short and frantically unfunny life attempting to protect Nature in the Delaware River Valley. He left his family without a cent. He had a criminal record, including flight from prosecution for a drug deal. But his most memorable crime was his violation of a law which has never been written down in so many words: "Monster fuck-ups engineered by your own government are not to be treated with disrespect until the damage done is absolutely unforgivable, incomprehensible, and beyond repair."

So much for "the right of the people peaceably to assemble, and to petition the Government for redress of grievances." (Or as a corrupt or stupid Head of State might put it, "If TV news is for me, who can be against me?")

I doubt that Abbie Hoffman's clowning shortened the Vietnam War by as much as a microsecond; nor did protests by anyone but the enemy. At a meeting of writers (P.E.N.) in Stockholm, when that war still had about a year to go, I said that almost all American artists of every sort were opposed to the war, forming a sort of laser beam of moral outrage. The power of this beam, I reported, turned out to be equivalent to that of a banana cream pie three feet in diameter when dropped from a stepladder four feet high.

My wife Jill ("Xanthippe") spent a whole year in Vietnam with the war going on. She photographed the Vietnamese people rather than the war stuff long before I met her. Some of those humane and beautiful pictures were combined with a text by Dean Brelis (then a CBS correspondent) in a book called *The Face of South Vietnam*. On her fiftieth birthday she received this letter from Brelis:

"Many happy returns, Jill.

"On this happy occasion, thoughts go back to nearly twenty-five years ago when you were in Vietnam. You did not get stuck on yourself. Not that anyone could blame a beautiful woman walking around like a queen, what with tens of thousands of men around. But you didn't. You hid behind those cameras of yours and you saw what so many did not see. You carried no gun—and more than one journalist did. You found the pain and the loss of the Vietnamese people, especially the children. You went deep into the nature of the cruel unhappiness brought to Vietnam. It often brought you to tears but you never gave up seeking out the truth. Behind every image you captured in Vietnam were your heart and your mind. And always your photographs asked, Why this? That question alone in your photographs was a good way toward finding the truth.

"It was a sad, grim land when you were there, Jill. The cities were burning, life had gone out of the villages, the paddy fields lay fallow, and I remember you cursing the human waste, the kids lying in the gutters. You shook your fist with rage, and then you went out with nuns and worked with them, picking your way through the garbage, to bring just a moment's warmth and hope where there was none. And very near, the Viet Cong watched and left you and the nuns alone. They knew you were easing the pain. Recently when I was in Ho Chi Minh City, which you knew as Saigon, one of those Viet Cong showed me a list of names of those round-eyes who were not to be harmed. Your name was on the list.

"Your actions and behavior in Vietnam, like your photographs, wanted a better world. I hope you feel a bit closer to that goal today as you begin to run to one hundred. As an old Vietnamese saying goes, the fun begins at fifty."

He signed the letter, "Your old pal, Dean Brelis."

So Xanthippe (Mrs. Vonnegut) is yet another saint.

Dr. Robert Maslansky, who treats every sort of addict at Bellevue Hospital in New York City, and in the jails, too, is a saint. (When we take walks together many homeless people greet him by name.) Tris Coffin and his wife Margaret, who get out a four-page weekly called *The Washington Spectator,* are saints. (I told Tris and Margaret a month ago that I considered them saints. They said they were too old to protest very vehemently.)

I can be more prompt than the Roman Catholic Church in announcing who is a saint, since I do not require courtroom-style proofs that so-and-so was on at least three occasions capable of magic with the help of God. It is enough for me if a person (like a good anthropologist) easily finds all races and classes equally respectable and interesting, and doesn't keep score with money.

Morris Dees, the southern lawyer who takes the likes of the Ku Klux Klan to court (thus putting his life on the line) on his own initiative, is a saint. (The Klan says he is a Jew, which he isn't. But what difference would that make?) I told him one time that he must be nuts, and he agreed. Ah me. Sure, and former Peace Corps people (now middle-aged) whom I met in Mozambique, who were working for the relief agency CARE there, are saints. They not only lived in friendly and shrewd harmony with the human beings they found there but taught them shipping and warehousing and accountancy (hard-edge business practices), so that starving to death might still be kept to a minimum after CARE went elsewhere (possibly to Leningrad).

Meanwhile, of course, back home (from the viewpoint of the CARE people), the forces of Beelzebub were waging racist and classist political campaigns, and taking over and liquidating businesses and natural resources, and looting pension funds, insurance companies, and savings banks, and putting a greater percentage of our citizens in jails and prisons than even the Soviet Union or the Republic of South Africa. (Some beacon of liberty we are to the rest of the world!)

XX

I said to the historian Arthur Schlesinger, Jr., one time, "If you had to say that the world was divided into only two kinds of people, not counting the sexes, what would they be?" It took him maybe ten seconds before replying, "Roundheads and Cavaliers." (I thought that was a swell answer. I am a Roundhead. Xanthippe is a Cavalier.) I said to the graphic artist Saul Steinberg one time, "There are some novelists I can hardly talk to. It is as though we were in two very unlike professions, like podiatry and deep-sea diving, say. What do you think is going on?" He replied, "It is very simple. There are two types of artists, neither superior to the other. One responds to life itself. The other responds to the history of his or her art so far." (Jill and I are both artists of the first sort, which could be why we got married. We are both barbarians, too ignorant to respond to the histories of our arts so far.)

Yes, and I, having just finished reading William Styron's short and elliptical account of his recent attack of melancholia, *Darkness Visible* (a suicide attempt may or may not have been involved), am now prepared to say that suicidal persons can be divided into two sorts. Styron's sort blames the wiring and chemistry of his brain, which could easily fit into a salad bowl. My sort blames the Universe. (Why mess around?) I don't offer this insight as yet another joke ("Why is cream more expensive than milk?"). It is my serious belief that those of us who become humorists (suicidal or not) feel free (as most people do not) to speak of life itself as a dirty joke, even though life is all there is or ever can be.

We do, doodily do, doodily do, doodily do
What we must, muddily must, muddily must, muddily must:
Muddily do, muddily must, muddily do, muddily must,
Until we bust, bodily bust, bodily bust, bodily bust.

(The summer of 1990 is just about finished, and so is this book. Christmas will be at our throats before we know it. My big brother Bernard says that the Christmas season makes him feel as though somebody were beating him in the face with a bladder.)

Shakespeare's Hamlet, when he sorts through the possible consequences of his doing himself in with a bare bodkin (sleeping pills and automobile exhaust and .357 Magnums were then unavailable), does not ponder the grief and confusion he might cause many who would still be alive. He was, after all, not only a close friend of Horatio and beloved by darling Ophelia, but the future King of Denmark. (The more recent abdication of Edward VIII from the Throne of England for the love of a gimlet-eyed divorcée from Baltimore comes to mind. My fellow novelist Sidney Zion said in mixed company at supper recently, anent Edward VIII, that blowjobs accounted for the history of the world so far. Some people are so *frank* nowadays!)

If Hamlet hoped to be remembered after he slammed the big door (or after somebody slammed it for him), I am sure he would have said so. Mark Twain (who wrote as though he would have liked to be remembered) said his reputation might outlive his body for at least a little while because he had moralized. (And indeed, his reputation has outlived his body.) I am sure he would have moralized in any case, but he had noticed that (for whatever reason) ancient writings which were still interesting in his day were all moralized. The anthology we call "The Bible" comes to mind. So should *Lysistrata* by Aristophanes (ca. 448–380 B.C.) and the Second Inaugural Address of Abraham Lincoln (1809–1865) and *Candide* by Voltaire (1694–1778) and *Heart of Darkness* by Joseph Conrad (1857–1924) and *The Theory of the Leisure Class* by Thorstein Veblen (1857–1929) and *Spoon River Anthology* by Edgar Lee Masters (1869–1950) and *Gulliver's Travels* by Jonathan Swift (1667–1745) and *Modern Times* by Charlie Chaplin (1889–1977) and on and on. So good advice to a young writer who wishes to circumvent mortality might be: "Moralize." I would add this caveat: "Be sure to sound reader-friendly and not all that serious when doing it." *Don Quixote* by Miguel de Cervantes (1547–1616) comes to mind. The sermons of Cotton Mather (1663–1728) do not.

Louis-Ferdinand Céline, the French fascist (and physician) about whom I wrote in *Palm Sunday,* may have tried to achieve a little immortality with deliberate, absolutely outragoeus immorality. I was talking to Saul Steinberg about Céline once, and I cried out in astonishment that a writer so funny and wise and gifted would intersperse what could have been masterpieces with loathsome attacks on Jews in general and, if you can believe it, jeers at the memory of Anne Frank in particular. "Why, why, why did he have to besmirch the sublimely innocent ghost of Anne Frank?" I said.

Steinberg pointed his right index finger at my breastbone. He said, "He wanted *you* to remember him."

(Steinberg is perhaps the most intelligent man in New York City. He may also be the most melancholy. He is far, far from home, having been born in 1914 Romania. He thinks the funniest joke in the world is this definition of an Irish homosexual: "A man who likes women more than whiskey.")

I don't care if I am remembered or not when I am dead. (A scientist I knew at General Electric, who was married to a woman named Josephine, said to me, "Why should I buy life insurance? If I die, I won't care what's happening to Jo. I won't care about anything. I'll be dead.")

I am a child of a Great Depression (just like my grandchildren). In a Great Depression any job is a miracle. Back in the 1930s, if somebody got a job there was a big celebration. Around about midnight somebody would finally inquire as to the nature of the job. A job was a job. To me writing books or whatever is just another job. When my cash cows the slick magazines were put out of business by TV, I wrote industrial advertising and then sold cars instead, and invented a new board game, and taught in a private school for fucked-up rich kids, and so on. I didn't think I owed it to the world or to myself or to anything to get back to writing, if I could. Writing was just a job I'd lost. When a child of a Great Depression loses a job, it is sort of like losing a billfold or a key to the front door. You go get another one.

(One jocular Great Depression answer to the question about what kind of job you got was, "Cleaning birdshit out of cuckoo clocks." Another one was, "It's in a bloomer factory. I'll be pulling down five thousand a year.")

Most people my age and of my social class, no matter what job they held, are retired now. So it seems redundant (even silly) for critics to say, as so many do, that I am not the promising writer I used to be. If they think I am a disappointment, they should see what the passage of time has done to Mozart, Shakespeare, and Hemingway.

The older my father was (and he died at seventy-two), the more absentminded he became. People forgave him for that, and I think people should forgive me, too. (I never meant anybody any harm, and neither did he.) Toward the end, Father actually called me Bozo several times. Bozo was a wire-haired fox terrier we had when I was a little boy. (Bozo wasn't even my dog. Bozo belonged to my big brother Bernard.) Father apologized for calling me Bozo. Ten minutes later he called me Bozo again.

During the last three days of his life (which I did not see) he would look through drawers and in cupboards for some sort of document. It was obviously important to him, but it was also a secret. He wouldn't tell anybody what it was. He never found it, and neither did we, so we will never know what it was.

(I can never forget the dying words of the actor John Barrymore, according to Gene Fowler in his *Good Night, Sweet Prince*: "I am the illegitimate son of Buffalo Bill.")

XXI

Many people feel that humor (professorial drolleries excepted) is a scheme of self-defense which only members of famously maligned and oppressed minorities should be allowed to use. (Mark Twain cast himself as poor white trash.) It must seem very wrong to them that I, an educated, middle-class person of German descent, should joke all the time. As far as they are concerned, I might as well be singing "Ol' Man River" with tears in my eyes.

(Saul Steinberg was talking one time about muzhiks, which is to say Russian peasants. I said that I had been a muzhik. "How could you ever have been a muzhik?" he exclaimed. We were sitting by my swimming pool in the Hamptons. I said, "I was a Private in the Army for three wartime years.")

In a wide-open seaport like New York City, where persons of all races and degrees of sophistication come (as during the California gold rush of 1849) to find fortune or doom, everybody sizes up everybody else largely on the basis of minute distinctions in race, usually (except where fear or anger is present) without saying so. Thus am I aware when talking to the writer Peter Maas, for example, that he is half Irish and half Dutch, or when talking to Kedikai Lipton (who is "Miss Scarlet" on the box for the Parker Brothers game Clue) that she is half Japanese and half Irish. When I talk to my best friend (now that the purebred Irishman Bernard V. O'Hare has joined the Choir Invisible) Sidney Offit, I am aware that he is Jewish.

So people must size me up as a German, because that is what I am. (At a bar mitzvah a couple of years ago, the movie director Sidney Lumet asked me if I was Dutch or Danish, and I answered silently but so he could read my lips, "Nazi." He laughed. I dated some with a really swell Jewish writer when my first marriage was falling apart, and I heard her tell a friend on the telephone that I looked like a Storm Trooper.)

People ask me how I feel about German reunification, and I reply that most of what we like about German culture came from many Germanys. What we have good reason to hate about it has come from one.

(What is really scary about Germans in Germany is that they enjoy fighting other *white* people. When I was a PW, one of our guards who had been shot up on the Russian Front mocked Britain's imperial military exploits. He said in English, "Them and their Neeger wars." If he is still alive, and has heard about Grenada and Panama and Nicaragua and so on, he could be laughing at *our* Neeger wars.)

The hatred for all things German expressed by Anglos in this country during World War I (before my birth) was so virulent that there were virtually no proudly German institutions still operating (I include my father) when it came time for World War II. German-Americans had become (in self-defense and in embarrassment over Kaiser Wilhelm and then Hitler) the least tribal and most acculturated segment of our white population.

(Who was Goethe? Who was Schiller? Ask Casey Stengel or Dwight David Eisenhower.)

One American in four is descended from German immigrants, but what politician nowadays ponders how to woo the German vote? (That is OK with me.) I am only sorry that the mostly German-American Freethinker movement did not survive the obliteration, since it might have become an extended family for the millions of good Americans who find all the big questions about life unanswered, save by ancient baloney of human manufacture. Before World War I, the Freethinkers had cheerful congregations, and picnics, too, in many parts of this country. If not God, what was there for them to serve during their short stay on Earth? Only one thing was left to serve under such circumstances, which was their community. Why should they behave well (which they did), quite certain as they were that neither Heaven nor Hell awaited them? Virtue was its own reward.

If there were Freethinker Societies today, lonely rationalists, children of the Enlightenment, wouldn't have to consider throwing away their brains, as though their heads were nothing but jack-o'-lanterns, in their desperate search for spiritual companionship.

I considered sandbagging the Appendix of this book with a long essay on Freethinking written by my great-grandfather Clemens Vonnegut in Indianapolis at the turn of this corrupt and bloody century. He was no holy man. He was a hardware merchant ("You can get it at Vonnegut's") who had done Occidental-style meditation, which consisted of reading books. His essay was as secular a creation as the Hippocratic Oath, which has governed the behavior of decent physicians for millennia. I have deposited copies of the essay in the New York Public Library and the Library of Congress, and let it go at that.

Here ends (to my astonishment) yet another book written not by somebody else but by me. (When I was living on Cape Cod

I had a carpenter build single-handedly a small ell on my house. When it was done he said the most wonderful thing. He said, "How did I ever *do* that?" Thus does the Universe continue to bloom or fester during its expansion phase. He wasn't the German mentioned in the Preface, the one who shot himself. He was Ted Adler, German for "eagle," born in the USA. He fought the Germans in Italy.)

In my very first book, *Player Piano* (published a mere thirty-eight years ago, before the perfection of transistors, when machines making human beings redundant were still enormous, doing their thinking with vacuum tubes), I asked a question which is even harder to answer nowadays: "What are people for?" My own answer is: "Maintenance." In *Hocus Pocus,* my last book before this one, I acknowledged that everybody wanted to build and nobody wanted to do maintenance. So there goes the ball game. Meanwhile, truth, jokes, and music help at least a little bit.

(The second-funniest clean joke in the world was told to me personally by the great comedian Rodney Dangerfield. We were in a movie together. He said he had a great-uncle who was admired for his cleanliness. He was the talk of the neighborhood. This old man took six, seven, eight, sometimes as many as twelve baths or showers every day. After he died, his whole funeral cortege went through a car wash on the way to the cemetery.)

Time to say yet again, *"Auf Wiedersehen."*

The person I have particularly in mind when I say that, of course (even though I know that life is a brief interval between black and black), is Bernard V. O'Hare.

Great-grandfather Clemens Vonnegut concluded his essay on Freethinking with a fragment from his own translation of a poem by Goethe. It seems no bad thing if I follow his example, to wit:

Subject to eternal,
Immovable laws,
We all must fulfill
The circles of our existence.
Man alone is able to do
What's seemingly impossible.
He discriminates,
Chooses and judges;
He can make the moment last.

He alone may
Reward the good,
Punish the wicked,
Heal and save,
Join to utility all
That's erringly rambling.

Appendix

WHAT MY SON MARK WANTED ME
TO TELL THE PSYCHIATRISTS
IN PHILADELPHIA,
WHICH WAS ALSO THE AFTERWORD
TO A NEW EDITION
OF HIS BOOK *THE EDEN EXPRESS*

The events described in *The Eden Express* took place nearly twenty years ago. Some things have changed. The notion that mental illness has a large biochemical component is no longer very radical. Things have come full circle, to the point where it's unusual to hear anyone say that mental illness is all mental. The view that going crazy is caused by bad events in childhood and that talk and understanding offer the best hope for a cure seems very out of date. This is a change for the better, although it has by no means brought an end to the shame, blame, and guilt which continue to compound the suffering of the mentally ill and their families.

The clinical definition of schizophrenia has been changed. Under the old definitions there was considerable ambiguity about what to call people like me. Under the new definitions I would be classified as manic-depressive rather than schizophrenic. I wasn't sick for very long and I didn't follow a downhill course, so I did not fit what has now become a definition of someone who is schizophrenic. While it's tempting to dismiss this as an insignificant change in labels and be more than a little irritated that they went and changed the rules after I went and built a book around the old definitions, I have to admit that this too is probably a positive change. It should mean that fewer people with acute breakdowns will be written off as hopeless. Eventually someone will develop a simple blood test that will sort out who has what disease and what treatments should work. In the meantime we're stuck with arguing about labels and indirect evidence as the best way we have of approaching useful truths about how to help people.

There are probably a dozen or so separate diseases responsible for what we now call schizophrenia and manic depression. Until the definitive work is done, many things are plausible and almost anything is possible. This lack of certainty makes mental illness wonderful ground for intellectual speculation and absolute hell for patients and their families.

At the time I wrote my book I felt that the large doses of vitamins with which I was treated, along with more conventional therapies, had a great deal to do with my recovery. It was my hope that many people diagnosed as schizophrenic would get better if only their doctors would become more open-minded and treat them with vitamins. Since that time I've seen people with breakdowns like mine recover every bit as completely as I did, without vitamin therapy. I've seen many cases where vitamin therapy didn't make any difference and a lot of cases like mine where it's hard to say exactly what did what.

I continue to feel a great deal of affection for the doctors who treated me. They were good doctors with or without vitamins, which they saw mostly as something that couldn't hurt and might help.

What I can no longer continue to do is maintain that vitamins played a major role in my recovery. I have not changed the text of my book, since I think it should stand as I wrote it. I remain very proud of the book, but if I could have one line back I'd delete "The more the vitamins took hold . . ." (p. 201). I'd also drop the paragraphs dealing with how to find out more about vitamin therapy in the postscript.

Life has been good to me. I made it into and through medical school and managed to enjoy myself most of the time. I practice pediatrics, which I continue to find very congenial, rewarding work. I have two healthy sons and am still in love with my wife. I'm surprised how much I care about the Red Sox.

I still think a fair amount about the sixties and trying to be a good hippie. I'm under no illusion that I understand exactly what was going on back then, but there are a few things that need saying. We were not the spaced-out, flaky, self-absorbed, wimpy, whiny flower children in movies and TV shows alleging to depict the times. It's true that we were too young, too inexperienced, and in the end too vulnerable to bad advice from middle-aged sociopathic gurus. Things eventually went bad, drugs took their toll, but before they went bad, hippies did a lot of good. Brave, honest, and true, and they paid a price. I'm sure no one will ever study it, but my guess is that there are as many disabled and deeply scarred ex-hippies as there are Vietnam vets.

When all is said and done, the times were out of joint. Adults as much as said that they didn't have a clue what should be done and that it was up to us, the best, bravest, brightest children ever, to fix things up. We gave it our best shot, and I'm glad I was there.

COMMENT

If well-educated hippies like Mark, who were in good health and of military age during the Vietnam War but did not risk their lives and honor in the slaughter, are indeed as scarred as those who fought, their wounds were of a different sort. Chief among these, I will guess, was shame about their membership in a social class (my class) so pandered to by the Government that its young (with a few exceptions) did not have to go to war if they didn't want to. I myself remember only one face and personality which went with a name on the Vietnam Veterans Memorial in Washington, D.C. They belonged to a physician's son who was a notorious screwup, whose parents thought he might be straightened out by Army discipline. The boy was back home again in no time, at permanent attention in a body bag.

I know only one other father, a prosperous potato farmer (on whose tennis court I used to play with Sidney Offit), who lost a son over there. He and his son (whom I did not know) were conventionally patriotic in the manner of almost all Americans during World War II, during which all social classes proudly shared sacrifices and great risks with something approaching equality. They thought it was not only a duty but a privilege for a young man to kill or be killed in time of war. I believed that, and was not mistaken to believe that during World War II. To have asked my parents to connive with politicians so as to get me an assignment well behind the lines would have seemed to me (and later to my children, too, if they had heard about it) unforgivable sleaze, which is to say a case of a conscience committing suicide.

Mark inherited a World War II conscience (as did O'Hare's kids, and on and on). So he had to maim if not kill it, if he was to stay out of the Vietnam nightmare, which must have hurt a lot. He, like so many members of his generation, became a man without a country because his Government was behaving in a manner toward the young of its own lower classes, not to mention the Vietnamese, which was not only cruel and hideously wasteful, but as I've said so often before, gruesomely ridiculous.

Mark did not like it here, nor should he have liked it. So although he was no longer subject to military service, or running from anything but a power structure (like the one today) shamelessly rigged in favor of his own race and economic and intellectual class, he went to Canada. All this is in *The Eden Express*. A sequel (and I hope he will write one, because he is such a good writer) would tell of his recovering sufficiently from a crack-up to go through Harvard Medical School and become a middle-aged pediatrician and saxophonist with two kids of his own, in group practice on the edge of Boston. (The nurses at

Massachusetts General Hospital recently named him their favorite pediatrician, and among his young patients was a grandson of my late friend Bernard Malamud.)

Mark's only crime against his government, and the only crime committed by Abbie Hoffman and so many others of that generation during the Vietnam War, was a sublimely Jeffersonian form of treason. It was disrespect.

I subtitled a novel of mine about World War II *The Children's Crusade*. But the average age of an American corpse in my war was an unchildlike twenty-six. In the Vietnam War your average American corpse was six years younger. So were the four antiwar demonstrators who were shot dead by the National Guard (draft-dodgers in uniform) at Kent State University in Ohio in 1970. Because the most visible of the antiwar protesters, who included many returned Vietnam veterans, were so young, all they stood for could be dismissed by their enemies as symptoms of immaturity. They were attempting to save lives and resources, but their appearance and manners (and music, and excitement and confusion about sex) made them unfit, so went the argument, for such a serious role.

I memorialized this prejudice in a plot scheme for a short story (never written) to be called "The Dancing Fool." I included the plot in a novel, and it goes like this:

"A flying-saucer creature named Zog arrived on Earth to explain how wars could be prevented, and how cancer could be cured. Zog brought the information from Margo, a planet where the natives conversed by means of farts and tap-dancing. Zog landed at night in Connecticut. He had no sooner touched down than he saw a house on fire. He rushed into the house, farting and tap-dancing, warning people about the terrible danger they were in. The head of the house brained him with a golf club."

If Abbie Hoffman had been my son, I would have told him that he was doing the right thing while the Vietnam War was going on. I would have warned him, too, that he was putting his life on the line for his countrymen.

"ON LITERATURE" BY KAREL ČAPEK, FROM *TOWARD THE RADICAL CENTER* (CATBIRD PRESS, 1990)

Forgive me if I start off with something quite other than literature, something from the days when I was a small boy. Your city boy is a kind of super-boy, a born skeptic, lord of the streets; and it is quite natural that he have a huge contempt for hayseeds, nincompoops, bumpkins, and clodhoppers, as he calls country boys. Your country boy looks down with immense and justified contempt on city boys, for he is lord of the fields and forests; he knows all about horses and is on friendly terms with the beasts of the field; he can crack a whip and he has under his dominion all the treasures of the earth, from willow-switches to ripe poppy-heads. And even your boy from a small country town is by no means the least among worldly princes, for he includes in his circle more than any other mortal creature: he can watch all human activities at close quarters.

When I was a boy in a small country town I saw at home how a doctor's business is run, and at my grandfather's I could inspect the business of a miller and baker, which is especially fine and amusing. And at my uncle's I saw what a farmer has to do; but if I started on that I would never stop telling you all the things I learned. Our nearest neighbor was the painter who stenciled designs on walls, and that is a tremendously interesting job. Sometimes he used to let me mix the colors in their pots, and once, almost bursting with pride, I was allowed to smear a stencil pattern with his brush; it came out crooked, but otherwise most successfully. I'll never forget how that painter used to stride up and down the planks whistling, gloriously splashed with all the colors of the rainbow; and he stenciled in such miraculously straight lines, sometimes even painting something freehand—perhaps an amazingly well-nourished rose the color of stale liver, on the ceiling. It was my first revelation of the painter's art, and I lost my heart to it then and have been in love with it ever since. And then I used to go every day and have a look at how the innkeeper does his job, to see how they roll casks down into the cellar and how they draw beer and blow off the froth, and hear the wise tales the old gossips tell as they wipe froth from their whiskers with the backs of their hands. Every day I would look in on neighbor cobbler and watch in silence how he cut leather and hammered it on his last and then put on the heel, and all manner of other things, for shoe-making is intricate and delicate work, and if you haven't seen leather in a cobbler's hands you know nothing about it at all, even if you do wear shoes of cordovan or even of celestial leather. Then there was neighbor hurdy-gurdy man, and I went to see him too, when he was at home, and was so surprised that he didn't play his hurdy-gurdy at home, but sat and stared at one corner of the room till I felt quite uncomfortable. There was the mournful stone-mason who carved crosses and strange, short, dumpy angels on gravestones; he'd tap away all day and never say a single word, and I'd stand watching for perhaps an hour while he chipped away at the unseeing eye of a weeping angel. And then, ha ha! yes! there was the wheelwright with his beautiful wood throwing off sparks and his yard full of hastening wheels, as Homer says; and a wheel, you know, is a wonder in itself. Then there was the smith in his black smithy: I burst with pride when I was allowed sometimes to work the bellows for him while, looking like a black Cyclops, he heated an iron bar red-hot and hammered it till it sent out a shower of sparks; and when he put a shoe on a horse it smelled of burnt horn, and the horse would turn his wise eyes on the smith as much as to say, "All right, go on, I won't make a fuss."

A little farther on lived Tonca, the prostitute; I didn't understand her business very well, and I used to pass her little house with an odd, dry feeling in my throat. Once I looked in through the window, but it was all empty—just striped featherbeds, and some consecrated pussy willows above the bed. I had a look at the mill owners' businesses, and watched them hurrying through their counting-houses, and collected foreign stamps out of their wastepaper baskets; and I watched the mill hands at the vats full of tow, and the weavers at the mysterious mechanical looms: I went into the red-hot hell of the jute-drying kilns and scorched myself beside the stokers at the boilers, wondering at their long shovels, which I could hardly lift. I would visit the butcher, eyeing him with interest to see if he would cut off a finger. I would have a look in at the shopkeeper as he weighed and measured; stop at the tinsmith's, and go into the carpenter's yard where everything was a-whirr and a-clatter. I went to the poorhouse to see what the poor do with themselves, and went with them to the fair in the city one Friday to learn how the business of begging was carried on.

Now I have a profession of my own, and I work at it the livelong day. But even if I were to sit on the porch with my work I don't think a single boy would come—standing on one bare foot and rubbing his calf with the other—and watch my fingers to see how a writer's business is done. I don't say that it is a bad or useless profession: but it isn't one of the superlatively fine and striking ones, and the material used is of a strange sort—you don't even see it. But I'd like all the things I used to see to be in it: the ringing hammer-strokes of the smith and the colors of the whistling housepainter, the patience of the tailor and the careful chipping of the stone-mason, the bustling of the baker, the humility of the poor, and all the lusty strength and skill which men of towering stature put into their work before the astonished and fascinated eyes of a child.

COMMENT

Scientists like my big brother Bernard, who is engaged in pure research, also have eyes which are childlike with astonishment and fascination. Bernard and I have such eyes in common. His wonderment, however, is reserved for the lusty strength and skill of whatever created the Universe. As I write this, I am confident that Bernard, although he is one hundred miles away and I haven't talked to him on the telephone for three days, is thinking about thunderstorms. He in turn can be confident that I am usually thinking about human wickedness.

But when I do Occidental-style meditation with this essay by Čapek, when I make the rest of the world drop away by gazing at little black marks on a printed page, I borrow Čapek's mind and am refreshed by its innocence. No matter where I look in his village, as long as I use his brain, not mine, I can see no wickedness. For this relief much thanks. Because it is such a relief to get away from one's own brain from time to time, books, despite television and all the rest of it, will continue to be popular with those who have done the hard work of learning to read easily.

I have just read a book called *The Death of Literature* by Alvin Kernan (Yale University Press, 1990). He is Avalon Professor of Humanities Emeritus at Princeton, and he is not kidding with his book's title. He offers a thousand scholarly proofs that literature is now as inert as Tutankhamen. He may be right about literature as a subject which can be taught without attracting political attacks in a university nowadays. But works of art are rarely if ever created with a classroom in mind. The clear intent of all sorts of nontheatrical artists is that their devices, be they books or paintings or serious pieces of music or whatever, become mantras, means for individuals to enter isolated states of meditation. Meditation has to be a solitary activity, so that anyone, no matter how charming and well informed, who asks meditators what they are feeling or tells them what they should be feeling is that variety of pest known as a kibitzer.

If I am apathetic about most academic critics of literature, the ennui is surely mutual. Whereas I find almost nothing of use to a working fiction writer in academic criticism, I have seldom met an academic critic at all interested in asking a writer why and how he does what he does. To me this is like a chemistry professor's being proud of snubbing the element oxygen.

Yes, and whatever the future may hold for literature in classrooms, uncounted millions of Americans will continue to meditate with books in perfect privacy, escaping from their own weary minds for at least a little while, leaving no record of having done so in the form of a term paper or three credit hours toward a baccalaureate.

WHAT BERNARD V. O'HARE SAID
ABOUT OUR FRIENDSHIP
ON MY SIXTIETH BIRTHDAY

At the end of a war soldiers who have become war buddies lie to one another and say they will keep in touch. Kurt and I, however, did not lie, and we have managed to be completely unsuccessful in avoiding one another since then.

This is somehow true, although before the war we had nothing in common in our backgrounds except that we were about the same age and smoked too much. What we have in common now derives unhappily from the war and happily from our relationship as old and close friends.

I first met Kurt when assigned by the Army to participate in a specialized training program which brought us together at Alabama Polytechnic Institute in Auburn, Alabama. The Army Specialized Training Program was shelter for the preppies of World War II. But it terminated prematurely, and we were transferred to the Infantry. And because neither of us understood maps or had any sense of direction, we were put to work as reconnaissance scouts. This is explanation enough as to the circumstances of our capture.

Our captors told us that "for you the war is over" and sent us to Dresden.

We lived in a slaughterhouse. In the firebombing of that city by persons we thought were friends it proved to be the best house in town.

We went back to Dresden after the war. I don't believe that either of us really expected to find it there or to discover that it existed in the first place. But, and in spite of our training as reconnaissance scouts, find it we did, albeit in a somewhat different form from the Jewel City of our memory.

It was uncomfortable being there the first time and it was uncomfortable being there the second time.

Except in generalities, we never presently talk about Dresden or the war. This probably is because when together we laugh too much.

We laughed excessively on our return to Dresden, hysterical laughter, I believe.

Both of us agreed that we could still smell the smoke and some other things.

We didn't spend much time there.

Russia was also part of our itinerary. We didn't spend much time there, either.

In some reviews Kurt has been characterized as a black humorist. Those reviewers wouldn't know black humor from Good Friday. They don't know that what they read is only his reaction to the sight of the world gone mad and rushing headlong toward Dresden to the hundredth power.

And they miss his message, in which he pleads that world governments found their rule on something more akin to the Sermon on the Mount than the preachings of those who lead the world to Armageddon.

There is certainly nothing wrong with a man like that. And if such thinking constitutes black humor, it's too bad there is not an epidemic of it.

I am glad Kurt and I did not die.

And I would go back to Dresden with him again.

Happy Birthday, Kurt.

COMMENT

The photograph that follows shows what O'Hare and I looked like at the end of World War II in Europe, in early May 1945.

We are very hungry, and have been in that condition since being captured by the Germans in late December 1944. O'Hare and I are at the extreme right. He has a foot atop a roadside bench. He, like the rest of us, is wearing bits of uniforms from several different armies. I am in the rear of the wagon, with the back of my head against the tailboard. We are all survivors of the firebombing of Dresden. The photograph was taken by Tom Jones, who a mere forty-five years later would come to hear my contribution to a series of lectures at the National Air and Space Museum in Washington, D.C. The series was entitled "The Legacy of Strategic Bombing."

The situation in the photograph Tom Jones took is this: We are somewhere in rural southeastern Germany, near the border with Czechoslovakia. Our guards have marched us from a suburb of Dresden into this wilderness and suddenly disappeared, leaving us on our own in a wholly ungoverned area which would not be occupied by the Red Army for about a week. We have found an abandoned Wehrmacht horse and wagon, which we have made our own. In my novel *Bluebeard* I described the valley we have just left behind. It is being stripped of everything edible, as though by a locust plague, by liberated prisoners of war like ourselves, by convicts, lunatics, concentration camp victims, and slave laborers, and by armed German soldiers. We are hoping to find the American Army, so that we can eat and then go home. That Army is on the west bank of the Elbe River, which is far away.

The owner of the camera that took the picture was Bill Burns, now a retired broadcasting executive in Kentucky. He is right next to O'Hare in the foreground. He, too, has a foot atop the bench. He found the camera in a ditch, along with discarded Nazi regalia and weapons and so on. There was a roll of unexposed film inside.

The man on the driver's seat, next to an approximation of an American flag, is Dick Coyle, now a high school teacher and football coach in Ohio. The man playing a harmonica, Jim

© *William Burns; courtesy of the photographer*

Donnini, is a retired builder in Florida. To the left of the American star painted on the side of the wagon, wearing a British paratrooper's beret, is Dale Watson. Behind the driver's seat, seemingly about to shade his eyes, is Dick Crews. I have no idea what has become of Watson and Crews, and so cannot say for certain that the first of the eight of us to die was O'Hare. I do assert that we could not have posed for that photograph in that May so long ago had it not been for the bravery and sacrifices of the common people of the Soviet Union. They fought the hardest, they suffered the most, and they broke the back of what was by far the largest part of the Nazi war machine.

It is time a monument was raised to those common people somewhere in this country, which is so much more fortunate. Throughout their history they have known little else than want and tyranny. And now famine is upon them and their children.

(O'Hare had it wrong about where we met, by the way. I never even heard of the Alabama Polytechnic Institute before I read what he wrote for the Festschrift, saying we had met there. He is gone now, and nobody is supposed to say anything bad about the dead. But still you have to wonder what else he got wrong.)

FROM "THE BOMBER'S BAEDEKER"
(GUIDE TO THE ECONOMIC IMPORTANCE OF GERMAN TOWNS AND CITIES, 1944)

DRESDEN (Saxony)

51°3' N.   13°45' E: 600 miles: (640,000)

Dresden, the capital of Saxony, is situated on both banks of the river Elbe, and stands at approximately 360 feet above sea level. The left bank, with the Altstadt, or old town, as nucleus is the larger of the two parts; in it are found the commercial centre, the residential area and public buildings, and some industries, mainly in its S-Suburbs. Neustadt, on the right bank, and its suburbs contain industrial centres and administration.

In peace time tobacco, chocolate, and confectionery manufacture played a large part in Dresden's industrial activity; there are also a large number of light engineering works and makers of machinery which are now engaged on all kinds of war production, many of which are too small to be listed individually. Several important factories are making electric motors, precision and optical instruments and chemicals.

The munitions workshops in the old arsenal occupy an extensive area to the North of Neustadt, along the railway to Klotsche, in the industrial region which extends past the aerodrome to the Dresdner Heide. In the Heide, a large heath, munitions are reported to be stored in quantities.

Dresden is an important railway centre. The main connections between South and East Germany and the direct line from Berlin to Prague and Vienna pass through Dresden whence several branch lines lead to Leipzig and other parts of industrial Saxony.

The river harbour is of considerable importance to the freight traffic of the Elbe.

To the SW. of the town in the valley of the Weisseritz is the industrial town of Freital (dealt with under its own heading) and a small coal field which supplies the light industries that have been developed in Dresden.

Along the northern bank of the Elbe between Dresden and Meissen are a number of industrial settlements which are outside the municipal area of Dresden. These have been dealt with separately under the town headings Radebeul, Coswig near Dresden, and Meissen.

COMMENT

This is a page from a sort of directory kept aboard British and American bombers, from which crews might pick targets on their own in case they hadn't been able to carry out their assigned mission that night or day. I reproduce it here to show that there wasn't much in the Dresden area worth bombing out of business according to our own Intelligence experts. So burning the whole place down wasn't an exercise in military science. It was religious. It was Wagnerian. It was theatrical. It should be judged as such.

Rest eternal grant them, O Lord,
and let light perpetual shine upon them.
A hymn befits Thee, O God, in Zion,
and to Thee shall be paid a vow in Jerusalem.
Hear my prayer,
to Thee all flesh shall come.
Lord, have mercy upon us.
Rest eternal grant them, O Lord,
and let light perpetual shine upon them.

A day of wrath, that day,
it will dissolve the world into glowing ashes,
as attested by David together with the Sibyl.
What trembling there will be
when the Judge shall come
to examine everything in strict justice!
The trumpet's wondrous call sounding abroad
in tombs throughout the world
shall drive everybody toward the throne.
Death and nature shall stand amazed
when Creation rises again
to give answer to its Judge.
A written book will be brought forth
in which everything is contained
from which the world shall be judged.
So when the Judge is seated,

whatever sin is hidden will be made known.
Nothing sinful shall go unpunished.
Death and nature shall stand amazed
when Creation rises again
to give answer to its Judge.
What shall I, a wretch, say at that time?
What advocate shall I entreat to plead for me
when scarcely the righteous shall be safe from damnation?
King of awesome majesty,
Who to those that are to be saved givest the grace of salvation,
save me, O fount of pity.
Recall, dear Jesus,
that I am the reason for Thy journey into this world:
Do not cast me away from Thee on that day.
Seeking me, Thou didst sit down weary.
Thou didst redeem me, suffering death on the cross:
Let not such toil have been in vain.
Just Judge of vengeance,
grant me the gift of pardon
before the day of reckoning.

I groan like one condemned;
my face blushes for my sins;
spare a suppliant, O God.
Thou who didst absolve Mary Magdalen,
and heard the prayer of the robber,
hast given me hope as well.
My prayers are not worthy;
but Thou, of Thy goodness, deal generously with me,
that I burn not in the everlasting fire.
Give me a place among the sheep,
and separate me from the goats,
setting me on Thy right hand.
That day will be one of weeping,
on which shall rise again from the embers

the guilty man, to be judged.
When the accursed have been confounded
and sentenced to acrid flames,
call me along with the blessed.
That day will be one of weeping,
on which shall rise again from the embers
the guilty man, to be judged.
Therefore spare him, O God.
Merciful Lord Jesus,
grant them rest. Amen.

O Lord Jesus Christ, King of Glory,
deliver the souls of all the faithful departed
from the pains of hell and from the bottomless pit.
Save them from the lion's jaws,
that hell may not engulf them,
that they may not fall into darkness,
but let St. Michael the standard-bearer lead them into the
    holy light
which Thou of old didst promise to Abraham and his seed.
Sacrifices and prayers of praise to Thee, O Lord, we offer:
Do Thou receive them on behalf of those souls
whom this day we commemorate.
Allow them, O Lord, to pass from death unto life.
Holy, holy, holy, Lord God of Sabaoth,
heaven and earth are full of Thy Glory.

Hosanna in the highest.
Blessed is he who cometh in the name of the Lord.
Hosanna in the highest.
A day of wrath, that day,
it will dissolve the world into glowing ashes,
as attested by David together with the Sibyl.
Hear my prayer,
to Thee all flesh shall come.

Merciful Jesus, who takest away the sins of the world,
grant them rest.
O Lamb of God, who takest away the sins of the world,
grant them eternal rest:

Let eternal light shine upon them,
O Lord with Thy saints forever, for Thou art merciful.
Deliver me, O Lord, from everlasting death on that
dread day when the heavens and earth shall quake,
when Thou shall come to judge the world by fire.
I am seized with trembling and I am afraid
until the day of reckoning shall arrive and the wrath to come.
Hear my prayer.
Deliver me, O Lord, from everlasting death.
That day, a day of wrath, calamity, and misery:
Rest eternal grant them, O Lord,
and let light perpetual shine upon them.

MASS PROMULGATED BY ME IN 1985

Rest eternal grant them, O Cosmos,
and let not light disturb their sleep.
A hymn is naught to Thee, O flying Stones,
nor a vow unratified
in a dream in Jerusalem.
Yet I pray:
From Thee all flesh did come;
Time, have mercy upon us;
Elements, have mercy upon us.
Rest eternal grant them, O Cosmos,
and let not light disturb their sleep.

A day of wrath, that day:
We shall dissolve the world into glowing ashes,
as attested by our weapons for wars
in the names of gods unknowable.
Let not the ashes tremble,
though some Judge should come
to examine all in some strict justice!
Let no trumpet's wondrous call sounding abroad
in tombs throughout the world
drive ashes toward any Throne.
Let ashes remain as ashes,
though summoned to approach in terror,
as in life, some Judge or Throne.
Must a written book be brought forth
in which everything is contained
from which the ashes shall be judged?
Then when some Judge is seated,

and whatever is hidden is made known,
let him understand
that naught hath gone unpunished.
Let Death and Nature say what they will
when ashes sleep like ashes
when commanded to give answers to some Judge.
What shall I, a wretch, say at that time?
What advocate shall I entreat
when even the righteous have been damned
by wars in the names of gods unknowable?

Structure of awesome majesty,
donor of sleep or wakefulness,
Thou fount of random pain or pity,
give me the innocence of sleep.

Gambler with flesh,
Thou art the reason for my journey:
Do not cast the dice again on that day.
My wild and loving brother
did try to redeem me by suffering death on the cross:
Let not such toil have been in vain.

I groan like one condemned;
my face blushes for my sins.
Spare a suppliant from more such wakefulness.
Thou who didst neither condemn nor forgive Mary Magdalen
and the robber on the cross
hast given me hope as well.
My prayers are unheard,
but Thy sublime indifference will ensure
that I burn not in some everlasting fire.
Give me a place among the sheep
and the goats, separating none from none,
leaving our mingled ashes where they fall.

That day will be one of comical disappointment
to any who hoped to see rise again from the embers
the guilty to be judged.
When the litigious have been confounded
and sentenced to comical disappointment,
count me among the gratified.
That day will be one of comical disappointment,
on which shall rise again from the embers
no guilty man or woman or child to be judged.
I depend on you to spare them, O Stones,
O Time, O Elements.
Grant them rest. Amen.

O Cosmos, O structure of awesome majesty,
deliver without exception the souls of the departed
from the pains of Hell and from the bottomless pit.
Save them from the lion's jaws,
that Hell may not engulf them,
that they may only fall into darkness which is still and sweet.
Dazzle them not with light promised in a dream to Abraham
     and his seed.
Sacrifices and prayers of praise to Thee, O Cosmos,
we have offered for millennia.
Reward us with Thy continued indifference to the destinies past
     death
of those souls whom we this day commemorate.
Life was sport enough!
Allow them to pass from death unto sleep.
Holy, holy, holy, Time and the Elements:
Heaven and Earth are full of Thy Glory.

Hosanna in the highest.
Humbled and amazed are he and she who have experienced life.
Hosanna in the highest.
A day of wrath, that day:

We shall dissolve the world into glowing ashes,
as attested by our weapons for wars
in the names of gods unknowable.
Thus I pray to Thee,
from whom all flesh did come.

Merciful Time, who buries the sins of the world,
grant them rest.
Merciful Elements, from whom a new world can be constructed,
    moist blue-green, and fertile,
grant them eternal rest.

Let not eternal light disturb their sleep,
O Cosmos, for Thou art merciful.
Deliver me, O Cosmos, from everlasting wakefulness
on that dread day when the Heavens and Earth shall quake,
when we shall dissolve the world into glowing ashes
in the names of gods unknowable.
I am seized with trembling and I am afraid
until the day of reckoning shall arrive
and the wrath to come.
Hence I pray.
Deliver me, O Cosmos, from everlasting wakefulness
on that day of wrath, calamity, and misery.
Rest eternal grant them, O Cosmos,
And let not light perpetual
disturb their harmless sleep.

LATIN VERSION OF MY MASS
BY JOHN F. COLLINS

Requiem aeternam dona eis, Munde,
neve lux somnum perturbet eorum.
Nihili vobis hymnus, Lapides volantes,
nihili votum irritum
in somnis in Jerusalem.
Attamen oro:
a te omnis caro venit.
Chrone, eleison.
Stoechia, eleisate.
Requiem aeternam dona eis, Munde,
neve lux somnum perturbet eorum.

In die irae, in die illa,
solvemus saeclum in favilla,
testimonio nostris telis, factis in bella
in nominibus deorum ignorabilium.
Ne favilla contremiscat,
etsi aliquis Judex sit venturus,
cuncta tamquam stricte discussurus!
Nulla tuba, mirum spargens sonum
per sepulcra regionum,
cogat favillam ante ullum Thronum.
Favilla permaneat favilla,
quamquam vocata cum terrore accedere,
sicut in vita, ad aliquem Judicem vel Thronum.
Liber scriptus proferendus est
in quo totum continetur,
unde favilla judicetur?

Tunc, cum aliquis Judex sedebit
et quidquid latet apparebit,
is intelligat quod nil inultum remanserit.
Mors et Natura dicant quidlibet,
cum favilla ut favilla dormiat,
jussa se excusare alicui Judici.
Quid sum miser tunc dicturus?
Quem patronum rogaturus,
cum etiam justi sint damnati
bellis in nominibus deorum ignorabilium?

Factura tremendae majestatis,
dator somni vel vigiliae,
tu fons fortuiti doloris vel pietatis,
dona mihi somnum innocentem.

Aleator carne,
tu es causa meae viae:
ne iterum jacias talos in illa die.
Frater meus, qui temere me amavit,
me redimere conatus est crucem passus:
tantus labor non sit cassus.

Ingemisco tamquam reus;
culpa rubet vultus meus:
supplicantem serva plure talis vigiliae.
Qui nec Mariam et latronem in cruce damnavisti
nec eis dimisisti,
mihi quoque spem dedisti.
Preces meae non sunt auditae,
sed sublimi negligentia efficies
ut perenni non cremer ullo igne.
Inter oves locum mihi praesta
atque haedos, nullos nullis separando,
relinquendo nostram favillam ubi cadet permixtam.

Ridiculosae frustrationis erit dies illa
sperantibus videre resurgentes ex favilla
reos judicandos.
Confutatis litigiosis,
ridiculosae frustrationi addictis,
numera me in delectatis.
Ridiculosae frustrationis erit dies illa
qua resurget ex favilla
judicandus—nec vir nec mulier nec natus—nemo reus.
Vos confido eis parcere, Lapides,
Tempus, Elementa.
Donate eis requiem. Amen.

Munde, factura tremendae majestatis,
libera animas omnium ad unum defunctorum
de poenis inferni et de profundo lacu;
libera eas de ore leonis,
ne absorbeat eas tartarus,
ut plane cadant in obscurum tranquillum et suave.
Noli caecare eas luce promissa in somnis Abrahae et semini ejus.
Hostias et preces tibi, Munde,
laudis obtulimus in milia annorum.
Dona nos tua perpetua negligentia fatorum,
quae sunt trans mortem, earum animarum quas hodie
    commemoramus.
Vita satis erat ludi!
Fac eas de morte transire ad somnum.
Sanctum, sanctum, sanctum, Tempus, et Elementa;
pleni sunt caeli et terra gloria vestra.

Hosanna in excelsis.
Humiliati et stupefacti ille et illa, qui vitam experti sunt.
Hosanna in excelsis.
In die irae, in die illa,
solvemus saeclum in favilla,

testimonio nostris telis, factis in bella
in nominibus deorum ignorabilium.
Sid ad te precor,
a quo omnis caro venit.

Pium Tempus, quod sepelis peccata mundi,
dona eis requiem.
Pia Elementa, a quibus novus aedificari potest mundus,
humidus caeruleus fertilis,
donate eis requiem sempiternam.

Ne lux perpetua somnum perturbet eorum, Munde, quia
     pius es.
Libera me, Munde, de vigilia aeterna
in illa die tremenda quando caeli movendi sunt et terra,
dum solvemus saeclum in favilla
in nominibus deorum ignorabilium.
Tremens factus sum ego, et timeo,
dum discussio venerit atque ventura ira.
Itaque oro.
Libera me, Munde, de vigilia aeterna
in illa die irae, calamitatis, et miseriae.
Requiem aeternam dona eis, Munde,
neve lux perpetua somnum innocentem perturbet eorum.

UNPUBLISHED ESSAY BY ME,
WRITTEN AFTER READING GALLEYS
OF AN ANTHOLOGY OF FIRST-RATE
POEMS AND SHORT PROSE PIECES
BY PERSONS WHO WERE OR ARE IN
INSTITUTIONS FOR THE MENTALLY ILL

There was a time when clerical workers, if they were of a mind to, were allowed to put up funny or even impudent signs on walls near their desks, and such signs could be bought in what were then called "five-and-ten-cent stores." One of these, I remember, was:

YOU DON'T HAVE TO BE CRAZY TO WORK HERE,
BUT IT HELPS.

I may have seen that prefab joke for the first time at the Vonnegut Hardware Company in Indianapolis, where I used to work in the summertime in order to pay for clothes, dates, and petroleum. The store was owned by another branch of the family.

Then as now it was widely held that a person doing remarkably fresh work in the arts actually had to be crazy. What mentally healthy person could have thoughts that unusual? For a brief time, when my father was a boy, it was believed that there was a connection between tuberculosis and genius, since so many famous artists had TB. The early stages of syphilis were also rumored to be helpful. And E. B. White, the late writer and great editor of *The New Yorker*, said to me one time that he didn't know of any male author of quality who wasn't also a heavy drinker. And now, as though we needed any further proofs that creative persons are beneficiaries of disease, we have this volume of first-rate writings by the formerly or presently or since dead mentally ill, none of them, however, famous.

To me, though, and I have been in the writing business for a long time now, this book proves only two things: first, that more good writing is being done than we can afford to publish and find time to read, and second, that creative people have thoughts unlike those of the general population because they have been culled or feel they have been culled from that general population. The sequestering of some of us in mental hospitals is simply one of countless culling processes which are always going on. Tuberculosis or syphilis or a felony conviction or membership in a despised race or faction or a bad appearance or a rotten personality can get you culled as surely as a fancy nervous breakdown.

In order to be remarkably creative, though, it is not enough for a person to be culled or feel culled. He or she must also be gifted, as are all the contributors to this anthology. I have taught creative writing to all sorts of student bodies, ranging from those at Harvard University to teenagers at a private school for the disturbed or learning-disabled. It is my conclusion that the percentage of persons with literary gifts is nearly the same for almost any sort of gathering. So I would be surprised if that percentage, always a small one, were significantly higher or lower in a mental institution.

Again: It is culling, whether real or illusory, rather than disease which is the source of inspiration. I would not be surprised, however, if it turned out that gifted people culled for mental illness have given the world more works of art worth saving than those culled for other reasons. That would make sense, since nobody can feel as steadily and alarmingly excluded from the general population as they have felt. The rest of us make them the World's Champions of Loneliness. The word *egregious* ("outside the herd") might have been coined for them.

I quote the poet Kris Kristofferson: "Freedom's just another word for nothin' left to lose." There find encapsulated the benefit to a gifted person of being culled. Having nothing left to lose frees people to think their own thoughts, since there is no longer anything to be gained by echoing the thoughts of those around them. Hopelessness is the mother of Originality.

And the three lovely daughters of Originality in turn, the granddaughters of Hopelessness, as this volume demonstrates, are Hope, the Gratitude of Others, and Unshakable Self-respect.

MY REPLY TO A LETTER
FROM THE DEAN OF THE CHAPEL
AT TRANSYLVANIA UNIVERSITY
ABOUT A SPEECH I GAVE THERE

Dear Dean Paul H. Jones—

Our friend Ollie sent me a copy of your letter to him, written immediately after my speech out there.

I am a fourth-generation German-American religious skeptic ("Freethinker"). Like my essentially puritanical forebears, I believe that God has so far been unknowable and hence unservable, hence the highest service one can perform is to his or her community, whose needs are quite evident. I believe that virtuous behavior is trivialized by carrot-and-stick schemes, such as promises of highly improbable rewards or punishments in an improbable afterlife. (The punishment for counterfeiting in Henry VIII's reign, incidentally, was being boiled alive in public.) The Bible is a useful starting point for discussions with crowds of American strangers, since so many of us know at least a little something about it. It has the added virtue of having for contributors at least two geniuses—Moses and Christ.

Jesus is particularly stimulating to me, since he noticed what I can't help noticing, that life is so hard most people are losers or feel like losers, so that a skill essential to most of us, if we are to retain some shred of dignity, is to show grace in defeat. That to me is the lesson he taught while up on the cross, whether he was God or not. And he was neither the first nor the last human being, if that is what he was, to teach that while in unbelievable agony.

As for the preaching of formal Christianity, I am all for it.

As you saw with your own eyes, I myself have done that, and have done it without pay here in Baghdad on the Subway at the Cathedral of St. John the Divine and St. Clement's Church. My St. Clement's sermon can be found at the end of my book *Palm Sunday,* which also contains my words at Lavina Lyon's funeral out that way.

What I can't stand are sermons which say that to believe in the divinity of Jesus is a way to *win.*

Fraternally yours,

© *William Burns; courtesy of the photographer*

THE END